# MISTAKEN IDENTITY

## THE CASE AGAINST THE ISLAMIC ANTICHRIST

*A Quick Study Book*

## S. DOUGLAS WOODWARD

Author of *The Next Great War in the Middle East,*
*Lying Wonders of the Red Planet* and co-author of *The Final Babylon*

# MISTAKEN IDENTITY

## The Case Against the Islamic Antichrist

A QUICK STUDY BOOK™

S. Douglas Woodward
Faith-Happens
Oklahoma City, OK

Contact the author at **doug@faith-happens.com**
Web site is **www.faith-happens.com**
FACEBOOK is Facebook/S Douglas Woodward
TWITTER is @doomsdaydoug

All scripture referenced is taken from the King James Version of the Bible unless otherwise noted.

Most photographs are from Wikipedia Commons. Copyright notices and sources are provided when identified by the source. Photographs and charts utilized are considered fair use.

© S. Douglas Woodward and Faith Happens 2016

ISBN-13: 978-1530790906

ISBN-10: 1530790905

Cover design by the author. Featured is the *Hagia Sophia* (Holy Wisdom) Istanbul's famous landmark, a cathedral of Byzantium completed in 537 A.D., which became the Imperial Mosque of the Ottoman Empire when Sultan Mehmed II conquered Constantinople in 1453.

Printed in the United States of America

# Acknowledgements

Thank you to all my friends, followers, readers, and supporters who are too many to mention. My thanks to my frequent interviewers, Kevin Clarkson, Larry Spargimino, Derek Gilbert, Josh Peck, Margie Cole, and Shannon Davis who help promote my books and provide feedback as well as encouragement.

A special word of appreciation goes out to Ann Christopher and Anna Swain who offer many words of reassurance.

Thank you to Linda Kay Barnett and to Linda Church at Prophecy in the News for including me in their ministry. And last but not least: thank you to my wife Donna who puts up with the endless hours I spend writing when I could be with her in something much more entertaining.

# CONTENTS

**INTRODUCTION: A FULL RESET ON FUTURIST ESCHATOLOGY**   3

**PART ONE: WHAT'S RIGHT WITH THE ISLAMIC ANTICHRIST THEORY**   5

   Introduction to Part One   5

   1. The Islamic Antichrist Theory builds on a futurist platform.   5

   2. IAT is Pre-Millennial and Dispensational.   5

   3. Richardson and Shoebat Profess a Passionate Evangelical Faith.   6

   4. IAT treats the scripture seriously.   6

   5. Richardson and Shoebat earnestly contend for the faith once delivered to the saints.   7

   6. IAT rightly raises alarm about Islamic terrorism and the dangers in radical jihadist beliefs.   7

   7. The spirit of Antichrist is visibly apparent today in radical Islam.   8

   8. IAT warns of the deception we encounter with Islam.   9

   9. IAT has enlightened us on the nature of Islamic prophecy.   9

   10. IAT discloses that Turkey will become a dominating power and seeks to regain status as a caliphate.   11

**PART TWO: WHAT'S WRONG WITH THE ISLAMIC ANTICHRIST THEORY**   13

   Introduction to Part Two   13

   1. IAT presents a scenario that excludes key scriptures and geopolitical realities. As such, it fails as the best scenario to fit "all the facts".   13

   2. Rome destroyed Jerusalem and the Temple (Daniel 9:26-27), whether Syrian conscripts were in the ranks of Rome or not.   21

   3. Old Testament references to "the Assyrian" as the enemy of Israel don't designate a Syrian Antichrist.   22

   4. IAT wrongly argues the empire of Antichrist has only a regional, not global span of control.   24

   5. Saudi Arabia (and Mecca) are mistakenly regarded as Mystery Babylon in Islamic Antichrist Theory.   27

   6. Turkey is mistakenly identified as the powerbase of the Antichrist.   31

   7. Meschech, Tubal, Gomer, and Beth-Togarmah: not just names for ancient Anatolia (Turkey)   35

   8. The Muslim Mahdi, the Dajjāl, and the Antichrist are confused.   39

   9. The War of Gog and Magog is not the same as Armageddon; Gog and Antichrist are not the same person.   41

   10. The Jews will never accept a Muslim as their promised Messiah.   43

## PART THREE: GEOPOLITICAL REALITIES CHALLENGING THE ISLAMIC ANTICHRIST THEORY     53

    The Situation in Syria     53

    1. Russia is smack dab in the middle of the fray.     54

    2. Shi'ites are dominating the northern Middle East.     54

    3. The United States is operating in a "back-peddling" mode.     55

    4. Turkey has been more foe than friend and feuds with Russia.     55

    6. The U.S. has rescinded its plan to force regime change in Damascus.     55

    7. Israel temporarily enjoys not being at the center of hostilities.     56

    8. Russia likely to use Syria to build a stronger presence in the region.     56

    9. Turkey could attempt to block Russia's moves, but won't.     57

    10. Oil continues to be the elephant in the room.     58

    Conclusion     58

## APPENDIX I: THE ARAB SPRING - FIVE YEARS LATER     59

    Overview     59

    Highlights of the Arab Spring     59

    U.S. Abrogation of Responsibility for the Middle East     61

    Conclusion: The Confrontation of the Century Lies Just Ahead     63

## APPENDIX II: HISTORICAL REFERENCES TO GOG AND MAGOG     65

## ENDNOTES     71

# *MISTAKEN IDENTITY:*

## *The Case Against the Islamic Antichrist*

# Introduction:
# A Full Reset on Futurist Eschatology

During the past ten years, the most significant variant to emerge within *Futurism*[1] is the theory the Antichrist will be Muslim. However, Islamic Antichrist theorists assert much more than merely identifying that *Islam* comprises the religious background of the *son of perdition* – also known as the "Beast", the "little horn", the "king of fierce countenance", and "the willful king" of Daniel 11. Islamic Antichrist Theory challenges most aspects of what a majority of Bible prophecy students believe about "end times". And many aren't aware of this fact.

The Islamic Antichrist Theory (IAT) constitutes a full-fledged reset on almost all elements of Futurism. IAT deconstructs who the Antichrist is, where his powerbase will be, what city he will establish as his capital, his relationship to "Mystery Babylon", and whether or not he is one and the same as the Mahdi or the Dajjāl (the "Dark Messiah" of Muslim eschatology - Al-Masīḥ ad-Dajjāl). IAT conflates the wars of the last days and the key personages of Gog and Antichrist. It also reduces the scope of Last Days' events to just the Middle East.

Two principal authors and lecturers have popularized this dramatically revamped prophetic scenario. One is **Joel Richardson,** the author of the best-selling book *The Islamic Antichrist (2009)*.[2] The other is his former colleague, co-author and self-proclaimed (one-time) Palestinian terrorist **Walid Shoebat** (before the alliance with Richardson, Shoebat was the author of *Why We Want to Kill You* – 2006).

Richardson and Shoebat have written other books separately and one together in 2008 (*God's War on Terror: Islam Prophecy and the Bible*). They speak frequently at conferences, are active bloggers and publish numerous articles. *World Net Daily's* Joe Farah published *The Islamic Antichrist* and has been a strong advocate of Richardson. Likewise, Shoebat has also had important benefactors having spoken at many conferences produced by others, in particular those hosted by the venerable Chuck Missler. Both Shoebat and Richardson have made appearances on popular TV programs like Sid Roth's *It's Supernatural.*

Because he is so highly regarded, Missler's endorsement has carried considerable weight with eschatology students. And he has taken up the subject himself, reckoning someone from Middle Eastern descent may in fact fulfill prophecies concerning the Antichrist. (See Chuck Missler's DVD, *Antichrist: The Alternate Ending, 2006*). Additionally, Missler's endorsement adorns the cover of one of Richardson's most recent books, *Mideast Beast (2012)*. Exactly how much of the Islamic Antichrist Theory Missler supports is not clear, but given it contradicts many points he has asserted in the past, it's likely he does not agree with every aspect of the position.

While it is doubtful that they see eye-to-eye on all topics, Shoebat and Richardson hold to the same essential assertions about the Muslim Antichrist. In this book I will address IAT as a single theory propounded by multiple spokespersons. On occasion, however, I will clarify if only one person appears to hold to a specific element of the Theory.

I also have written on several facets of the Islamic Antichrist Theory (IAT) in my previous full-size book, *The Next Great War in the Middle East: Russia Prepares to Fulfill the Prophecy of Gog and Magog* (January 2016, 272 pages). This *Quick Study Book*™ "stands on its own"; nevertheless, it supplements the aforementioned prequel by focusing on several deeper elements of IAT.

Why did I do this? After interacting with many eschatology enthusiasts on social media over the last few months, I grew convinced it was necessary to dive deep into the subject matter and present additional analyses since so many have been persuaded by Islamic Antichrist Theory, which (from my viewpoint) errs on a number of crucial issues as hinted at above (and to be discussed in detail later). But to elaborate as introduction here, IAT contends there is:

*(1) No distinction exists between the Antichrist and the infamous person we know as **Gog** identified in Ezekiel 38-39, leader of a massive confederation attacking Israel.*

*(2) No distinction exists between the War of Gog and Magog and the War (or campaign) of Armageddon.* Richardson and Shoebat argue only one "last days" lies war ahead conflating Gog/Magog with Armageddon. No Psalm 83 war will occur.

*(3) A limited geographical scope in which end times' prophecy occurs.* Since I assert God judges the United States prior to end of the Tribulation, possibly when the War of Gog/Magog begins, reducing the scope of end times' prophecy to *regional wars* amounts to no small thing.³

Therefore, this book and its prequel were written to take issue with this widespread but incongruent view, that misinterprets the nature of Antichrist, his religious "affiliation", and the events occurring in the last days leading up to the return of Jesus Christ and the Millennium that follows.

Why this matters: students of Bible prophecy should care a great deal about this subject because so many truths about eschatology to which believers have held for so long have been forsaken by many and especially those that are new to the study of Bible prophecy. *What you have believed has been rejected and replaced by new ideas.*

Additionally, because Islamic Antichrist Theory sees Islam as the final world religion and the religion of the Antichrist,

**Joel Richardson and Walid Shoebat, Proponents for the Islamic Antichrist**

Christians may come to an erroneous fear and loathing of Islam. Make no mistake: *fanatical Islam is dangerous.* And any religion that denies the Father and the Son is a religion whose spirit is Antichrist. (1 John 2:22) *However, this is not the same as saying that Antichrist is Islamic – or that all Muslims are of Antichrist.* This distinction must be made lest as Christians we wrongly accuse good people of evil, when in many cases their fault lies only in *not yet understanding and professing faith in the true God and who He actually is* – as made known to us through Jesus Christ our Lord.

# Part One:
# What's Right with the Islamic Antichrist Theory (IAT)

## Introduction to Part One

WHILE I TAKE A STRONG POSITION AGAINST THE ISLAMIC ANTICHRIST THEORY (IAT), IT'S IMPORTANT TO BEGIN BY RECOGNIZING THE MANY BELIEFS I SHARE WITH MOST IAT PROPONENTS. Yes, there are strong reasons I disagree; however, I fully endorse the attempt to study the scripture with a fresh set of eyes and determine if any given "majority position" deserves modification. To be sure, my own views previously expressed in a dozen books, assert some variance with conventional eschatology advanced by popular writers, researchers, and scholars. This is especially so regarding my conviction that the United States plays a pivotal role in the "Last Days". So I wish to begin in this critique by noting *where I agree with IAT,* and *by expressing respect* for those who espouse the Islamic Antichrist perspective. The following topics summarize ten specific, critical areas *where we agree:*

## 1. The Islamic Antichrist Theory builds on a futurist platform.

Most Christians interested in Bible prophecy are *Futurists,* believing major events foretold by the Bible will be fulfilled in the years ahead. We see Bible prophecy and its fulfillment as one of the most important apologetic methods evangelists employ to demonstrate the Bible is a source of truth. We argue the Bible even challenges other religions **to predict the future as only the Word of the Lord can do.** *"Declaring the end from the beginning, and from ancient times the things that are not yet done, saying, 'My counsel shall stand, and I will do all my pleasure'"* (Isaiah 46:10, KJV). *Futurists* take the opposite perspective, as do *Preterists,* who argue biblical prophecy regarding the person of Antichrist, the War of Armageddon, and the Millennium are not future events awaiting a "space-time" fulfillment – these events have already taken place and thus are now "past tense". (Note: I prefer using "space-time" as an adjective in place of the word *"literal"* to describe how Bible prophecy is accomplished)[4]. Preterists often *spiritualize* elements of Futurist eschatology – meaning they see prophecies as nothing more than as metaphors and "myth" to be understood *allegorically,* that teach only existential truth and never culminate in future historical fulfillment in the everyday realm of space-time. It's no accident that Preterists often redirect prophecies intended for Israel and reapply them to the Church. Hence Preterism often goes hand-in-hand with what is often termed *Replacement Theology* (meaning: the Church *replaces* Israel in biblical prophetic discourse).

## 2. IAT is Pre-Millennial and Dispensational.

IAT adheres to the doctrine of the millennial reign of Christ on this earth and is aligned with an overall dispensational framework. Dispensationalism declares that we can best understand the relationship of God and humankind by citing distinctive periods, usually numbering seven discrete eras. Like standard theory, Islamic Antichrist theorists appear to hold the same hermeneutic traditions as conventional Pre-Millenarians.

However, the *timing of the Rapture of the Church,* i.e., the question of the Pre-Tribulation versus Post-Tribulation and/or Pre-Wrath Rapture positions, remains a separate question for IAT adherents. When asking him directly, Richardson chose not to elaborate much on the matter of the timing of the Rapture but indicated that he is not Pre-Tribulational in outlook. I suppose Shoebat is "Pre-wrath" or "Post-Trib" from various comments I've read in his materials.

### 3. Richardson and Shoebat Profess a Passionate Evangelical Faith.

Both authors hold to the essential doctrines of the Christian faith. From what I have studied, there does not appear to be any reason evangelicals should be concerned about their core Christian affirmations whatsoever. Shoebat and Richardson are true brothers in the faith. I also judge them smart, sincere, and assert they have accomplished much good for the Kingdom of God.

However, to the extent that they have misunderstood eschatology, to that extent they have brought (predictably) confusion into the fold. Of course, one cannot pursue *any* alteration to accepted theories *without unsettling the standard point of view*. Advancing our learning and understanding of the Scriptures comes with this risk. *No penalty should ever be ascribed for that effort.* Having said that, good intentions and prayerful methods do not automatically protect teachers from making big mistakes to the detriment of the fold. Thus, humility should always play a part when promoting any new understanding that differs with conventional thinking. And teachers should be accountable to other teachers in the field who are in the position to judge their contribution.

### 4. IAT treats the scripture seriously.

IAT attempts to understand what the scripture actually teaches. Richardson and Shoebat critique the conventional view (such as I generally hold) because they believe standard eschatology regarding who the Antichrist is and what Mystery Babylon comprise erroneous teachings – primarily since the interpretation concluded by *conventional teachers and scholars* are judged by Islamic Antichrist theorists to be mistaken based upon their conventional, *occidental* ("Western World") stance or worldview, with faulty assumptions about the nature of the Bible. In contrast, Islamic Antichrist theorists argue the Bible is a "Mediterranean" or *oriental* book and Western premises *are more likely to mislead than to inform.* They maintain that the only way one can correctly understand the Bible is by adopting a Jewish or "Middle Eastern" viewpoint. [I would take exception to this premise believing it is overstated – only partially true.]

In some cases, IAT criticism could be characterized as denigrating their opposition by characterizing conventional theory (more or less) as "pop theology", owing to views informed primarily by popular writings like the classic *Late Great Planet Earth*, and by the *Scofield Reference Bible* (with its famed "below the line commentary"), both which help construct the conventional theory that identifies who the Antichrist is, who or what Gog and Magog are, the distinctions between the various wars of the end days, and wrong-headed notions (from their perspective) regarding Mystery Babylon and the essence of the "beast system". While Scofield certainly had an enormous impact on evangelicalism in England and America, Richardson (in particular) may be giving Scofield too much credit and Hal Lindsey and Tim LaHaye too little. Dispensational theology was popularized in the first half of the twentieth century by such writers and teachers as G.H. Pember, C. I. Scofield, Clarence Larkin, and Robert D. Culver (among others), while the second half of the twentieth century thinking was influenced more by M.R. DeHaan, Finis Dake, John F. Walvoord, Donald Grey Barnhouse, Dwight W. Pentecost, Frank Logsdon, Hal Lindsey, Tim LaHaye, Grant Jeffrey, Chuck Smith, and J.R. Church, and Chuck Missler.

These are just a few of the many names supporting the conventional view of the Antichrist, his coming, his empire, his powerbase, his belief system, his revealing, and his role in the War of Armageddon which would be in opposition to IAT theorists. We will provide more information about the conventional theory, but more specifically how it has been revised during the past decade during the same timeframe as the Islamic Antichrist Theory has grown in acceptance. At this juncture, the issue to underscore is *how these two viewpoints are not compatible; indeed, they are highly contradictory.*

## 5. Richardson and Shoebat earnestly contend for the faith once delivered to the saints.

No one should question the ardor of Richardson or Shoebat to establish the truth about what the Bible teaches. As far as I am able to discern, they are "for real". As to Richardson, I make this judgment in part based on personal interaction. During a recent low-key debate with Joel, I learned a number of things concerning his beliefs and his ministry as well as his hope to reach Muslims and the Middle East for Christ. On the other hand, there are those that question whether Shoebat presents himself truthfully. They question whether he was in fact a terrorist for the PLO as he claims. Also, from insider information, I know he broke fellowship with the prominent WND publisher, Joe Farah. Also, according to Richardson, Joel has not collaborated with Shoebat for over four years. As to Shoebat's general standing in the evangelical community, I cannot speak to that.

As to passion: zeal in and of itself does not vouchsafe ANY man's arguments. As Paul said concerning the Jews of his day, *"I testify about them that they have a zeal for God, but not in accordance with knowledge"* (Romans 10:2, NASV). Whether IAT is right or wrong has nothing to do with the zeal of those who advocate its views. Indeed, most Americans mistrust ardent advocates, judging them just as likely to be wrong as right. Neither writer-teacher seems disingenuousness. Indeed, just the opposite seems to be the case. I assume they are remain sincere.

## 6. IAT rightly raises alarm about Islamic terrorism and the dangers in radical jihadist beliefs.

If the LORD tarries for two or more decades, the possibility that the spirit of Antichrist in Islam will have a drastic impact upon Christianity, even in America, is unquestionable. Short of a reformation in Islam (which a few moderate Muslims seek), the possibility that there could be true religious wars and armed crusades is not beyond reason. We are likely to see hate groups in America specifically targeting Muslims. Terrorist actions in America engender this reaction. As jihadists commit more terrorist acts – and they no doubt will

– it becomes ever more likely there will be skirmishes between anti-Muslim groups and Muslims. Additionally, the lack of assimilation of those committed to Islam in most Western cities, proffers an omen that a clash of cultures will soon lead to armed conflict, in Europe and in the Western Hemisphere. How this could come to be organized is unclear. Living peaceably in American cities, when sections of the cities become exclusively Muslim, will no doubt incite divisiveness – the "us vs. them" mentality. Should "no-go zones" develop in American cities due to Muslim animosity, tensions with non-Muslims will dramatically intensify, promising extensive violence. This issue should be taken up by cities now to blunt such confrontations in the years ahead. Will communities be proactive? Can Christians and Muslims work together to establish mechanisms to keep peace and dissuade rival gangs, civil riots, and general unrest in cities with large Muslim populations?

## 7. The spirit of Antichrist is visibly apparent today in radical Islam.

With 1.2 billion Muslims globally, and the orthodox view of Islam decidedly against the core concept of Christianity (that God is our Heavenly Father and Jesus is the Son of God), the danger that this religion will become a force for the antichrist spirit, by definition, intensifies year by year. For all believing Muslims, the denial of God as Father and of the Christian contention that Jesus is God's unique Son (incarnating the Father in human flesh) remains an element of Islam that is *non-negotiable* for Biblical Christians, just as the Christian view is non-negotiable for Islam. Paraphrasing a saying from Islam, "God is not our father and therefore He has no son." Of course, this affirmation constitutes almost verbatim what the New Testament teaches is the nature and sentiment of the antichrist spirit: *"Who is a liar but he that denieth that Jesus is the Christ? He is antichrist, that denieth the Father and the Son. Whosoever denieth the Son, the same hath not the Father: he that acknowledgeth the Son hath the Father also."* (1 John 2:22)

For those that teach that Allah and Jehovah comprise the same God, they are not just poorly informed, they are either deceived or they are intentionally oblivious to the fundamental teachings of Islam and Christianity.[5] Liberal (supposedly broad-minded, politically correct) Christians argue that revering Allah is just as viable as revering Jehovah. For both religions, asserting that the Gods are the same is unacceptable. *Finding common ground cannot be based on saying that we worship the same God. It must be based on saying that both God's demand similar values.* The history of Islamic religious history and theology as well as their own traditions and creeds rule out accepting either the Jewish or the Christian notion of God as Father. The assertion that orthodox Islam is a religion of peace constitutes another denial of history. There must be a distinction drawn between Salafist Islam (with Sunni or Shia) and Islam that has forsaken jihad, honor killings, deceiving infidels, and practicing Sharia law that contributes the "due process" of Western law. If these maxims cannot be acknowledged and accepted by both religions and their respective communities, there is little hope that the two religions and their adherents can live together in peace. Unfortunately, the number of Muslims willing to accept these rules likely numbers only slightly over 50%.

Would that the vast majority of Muslims were moderate monotheists. However, Muslims who *adhere strictly to the Quran and the hadiths* will never accept there is such a thing as "moderate Islam". That expressed point of view in the Media, promoted by Western politicians, and advocated by popular progressive opinion, has a very difficult time accumulating compelling evidence that it conveys any semblance of truth. Orthodox Muslims support Sharia law, jihad as a means of converting or eliminating infidels, while as many as 50% of the Muslim world continues to support honor killings and the suppression of women's rights. The notion that a caliphate should be established and followed by faithful proponents of Islam stands as a threat to world peace. The sooner that the Western World "gets real" and comes to grip with the reality of fundamentalist Islam and that 50% of Muslims hold to that view in the world today, the sooner that some sort of movement can be made to create a world where both religions and their respective communities can feel safe with one another. However, given the fabricated views that our press and politicians continue to press upon the public, the prognosis to make real progress does not look very good.

One of the great mysteries of our day is why progressives seem so naïve about the nature of the Islamic religion. They fervently support women's rights, but give Islam a pass on its horrific record for oppressing women. Neither Muslims nor Christians have found a way to *adopt toleration of the other without feeling they have compromised orthodoxy*. Mainline American Christians tout toleration but that compromise orthodoxy. Orthodox Muslims speak of toleration but actions betray their affirmations smack of disingenuousness.

## 8. IAT warns of the deception we encounter with Islam.

As expounded by Richardson and Shoebat, lying in order to harm its adversaries is fully condoned and considered ethical in Islam. Westerners remain highly adverse to any group or person that teaches lying is acceptable behavior. Since Islam has a core doctrine that it is okay to lie to infidels to further the cause of Islam, building trust between Muslims and Christians seems hopeless without some modification of Islamic adherence to this doctrinal position.

Of course, this ordinance is mild compared to the doctrine that infidels should be beheaded for their unbelief. (See the endnote for further elaboration on this topic).[6]

IAT theorists are correct to inform Christians that what Muslims say concerning their acceptance of Christians and toleration for the Christian faith is just as likely to be wrong as right. Westerners must come to terms that Islamic teaching, orthodox doctrine, must be repudiated by Muslims before their can be a "social compact" that can be relied upon by communities in the West. Is this likely to occur anytime soon? Without some movement at a high level in Islam to alter such teaching, mistrust between Muslims and Christians will continue and understandably so.

## 9. IAT has enlightened us on the nature of Islamic prophecy.

Richardson and Shoebat have informed evangelicals that the prophecies of Islam identify several iconic figures in the end times: Jesus (Isa), Antichrist (Dajjāl), and the Mahdi. While IAT theorists might judge the Mahdi to be the "False Prophet" of Revelation, on the surface there are some views in Christian and Islamic eschatology that they appear to hold in common. We share in a concept of a 3.5-year and 7-year period important to last days' chronology (which mimics Daniel's 70th week of years, or *shabuwa*). Does the fact that Islam shares some apocalyptic elements with Biblical Christianity imply a supernatural force is at work to mislead us? Not necessarily.

**Cover, *God's War on Terror***

We will learn a bit later that a portion of Islamic eschatology comprises nothing more than a rehash of a "trifle" from extra-biblical (non-canonical) extant writings known as "The Last Roman Emperor". These writings came centuries after the New Testament. Some of these spurious notions were embedded in the *hadiths, or sayings* attributed to Mohammed.

The Islamic Jesus, called *Isa* in Islam, is prophesied to come and testify on behalf of Mohammed as well as Allah. However, he will clarify that he is NOT the Christ as depicted in Christianity. Notably, he is assuredly NOT the Son of God. [Interestingly, it is this lesser Islamic *Isa* (Jesus) who defeats the Dajjāl (the Muslim version of antichrist)]. Islamic Antichrist theorists theorize this *Isa* might be the False Prophet in Christian Bible prophecy. However, he would *not* be the *Mahdi* (their equivalent of Messiah). But a caution is in order here.

Richardson and Shoebat seem to suggest some elements of Islamic prophecy may come to pass when in fact, if they came to pass the reality is that they would add to Islamic deception. Specifically, the personages identified by Islam and the God they supposedly represent is not likely to be consistent with what they contend. *"For false christs and false prophets will arise and perform great signs and wonders"* (Matthew 24:24). It could be very confusing to Christians who have been instructed by Islamic Antichrist theorists to treat the Islamic personages as the opposite of what they say about themselves. There is no guarantee they can be treated as "opposite" to what Islam says. *In other words, don't assume the Dajjāl is really Christ or a Christian prophet.* As mentioned above, Christians should be informed that much of Muslim eschatology, even aspects of the Mahdi, is plagiarized from Christian *pseudepigrapha* (pronounced, "sued pee graph ah") written sometime not before the fifth century. In other words, Christians should not anticipate a "literal" fulfillment of Islamic prophecy, just because it tracks to some aspects of biblical prophecy. It does so because, basically, it was *plagiarized*.

Wikipedia defines *pseudepigrapha* as works written and falsely attributed to someone else. Frequently, they are also known as *apocryphal* writings.[7] Researcher and author Chris White provides an insightful study into writings about the "Last Roman Emperor" (which we will study later), and how the descriptions of his conjectured reign mirrored Islamic conceptions of the Mahdi. White's book is entitled *The Islamic Antichrist Debunked*.[8] White's study on this *the Last Roman Emperor* is a fascinating and crucial subject to consider.[9]

## 10. IAT discloses that Turkey will become a dominating power and seeks to regain status as a caliphate.

IAT argues that the Ottoman Empire will be revived. They rightly warn us that Turkey, despite being a member of NATO, could become a very dangerous regional power, particularly given that their President Recep Tayyip Erdoğan, who has on at least one occasion confirmed that, "There is no such thing as 'moderate' Islam." Indeed, Turkey comprises a growing regional power. From most reliable sources, despite statements to the contrary, Turkey currently supports ISIS and other Syrian rebel groups in their attempts to overthrow the government of Bashar al' Assad. Turkey has been very duplicitous maintaining its relationship with the West (through NATO) while also seeking to return to Islamic Sharia Law – a difficult path to say the least, maintaining balance with Western alliances while attempting to incorporate laws that could conflict with Western decrees, regulations, and values. What is most damning and injurious: Erdoğan's facilitating ISIS shipping and selling oil with Turkey officially denying it.

Indirectly, Turkey enables the financing of ISIS and Jabhat al' Nusra, Syria's Al Qaeda affiliate (by which ISIS has realized in the recent past tens of millions of dollars in monthly revenues). While this situation may still exist today, political pressure from Washington and other NATO members may alter Turkey's behavior soon. Of course, to the extent that European nations benefit from the flow of ISIS oil, it isn't hard to believe that official policy and ongoing practice may have little in common.

Additionally, it should be noted that Turkey militarily assaults the West's primary ally in the region, the Kurds, due to an ongoing civil war. Turkey's recent participation in the shelling of rebel groups has proven for the most part to be a cover for its ongoing attack of the Kurds. This remains highly contradictory to Turkey's alliance with Western coalition members who see the Kurds as their strongest and most effective ally in fighting ISIS and indirectly, Bashar al-Assad's "regulars" (formal army). The U.S. continues to publicly denounce Assad and may have made an agreement behind closed doors with Russia to allow Assad to continue for the time being, in exchange for the U.S. lifting of sanctions and/or relaxing pressure on U.S. and E.U. moves against Russia over Moscow's annexation of Crimea and domination of Eastern Ukraine. Although the U.S. has demanded a "regime change" in Syria (seeking the ouster of Assad), as this book goes to press, the U.S. position has softened with the U.S. agreeing to cease covert operations and bombing to expel Assad.

Some political scientists such as George Friedman of *Geopolitical Futures* assert that Turkey will become an impressive economic power during the decades that lie ahead, accumulating capacity to influence Eurasia and its geopolitics. Just "how dominant" remains to be seen as Turkey is not without regional competition (Russia and Iran), and does not represent a stable democracy in several respects. Erdoğan faces considerable internal opposition and Turkey continues to incur substantial terrorist threats from the Kurds and possibly from ISIS.

Erdoğan continues to seek increased executive power by pushing for changes in Turkey's constitution. He strives for an autocracy, which he believes will better suit his goal for an Islamic caliphate with himself at the head. So far, he has been unsuccessful in reaching his ultimate goal, but his quest for greater executive control of the government continues to show progress with each major national election (his party continues to gain seats in Parliament, a super majority being needed to change the constitution). Also, it is not accidental that some are ready to proclaim Erdoğan possesses divine qualities, which seems most ironic inasmuch as this status would conflict with religious teachings in Islam (only Allah is divine – his prophet, Mohammad is not divine either, although the Prophet has a unique status). [10]

Finally, during the time writing this book, Turkey and Saudi Arabia amassed conventional weapons and thousands of troops on the Iraqi and Syrian borders conducting war games. Many observers worried the region could be on the cusp of a major war of Shia versus Sunni, a war that could involve Russia and potentially the Western coalition. Some have stated that this stand off will soon lead to World War III. As March 2016 came to a close, the Russians retired some forces from the region, while the U.S. kept its word not to forcibly oust Assad, and the ad hoc alliance of Turkey and Saudi Arabia decided against launching a ground attack in Syria. These latter two nations remain mired in their own internal politics. Additionally, there are so many violent conflicts within and surrounding their own borders it seems unlikely they would be in a position to supply major direct military assistance to the rebels in Syria.

Will the rebels rebound? It is likely they will. Only a far more decisive ground force pressing the attack across the region, combined with continuous air support from either Coalition forces or Russia, will eradicate all elements of ISIS in the area. Given that the Sunnis, both in Saudi Arabia and Turkey, want Assad expelled entirely (while Iran and Iraq prefer to see him stay), to say the least, there is no consensus to resolve the problem and no political solution on the horizon to satisfy the rebels.

Politically, Sunni adherents in Western Iraq must forge an agreement with regional Shia governments and the Alawite faction in Syria to end the war. Turkey, Iran, and Syria (however stable Syria is at the time) must establish sufficient order to eliminate ISIS from enjoying any geographical "state" or stronghold in the region that lies between Damascus and Baghdad. For the moment, neither Russia nor the Western coalition has come to the conclusion they are willing to press the fight to extinguish ISIS (that is, applying ground forces or supporting others who would do so). Until then, it is highly likely ISIS will continue to operate and threaten the Middle East.

But, if Turkey amasses more power and prestige without provoking Russia to war, it's conceivable Turkey could be instrumental in bringing about peace – but not likely.

# Part Two:
# What's Wrong with the Islamic Antichrist Theory

## Introduction to Part Two

IN MY MOST RECENT "FULL-SIZE" BOOK, *THE NEXT GREAT WAR IN THE MIDDLE EAST: RUSSIA PREPARES TO FULFILL THE PROPHECY OF GOG AND MAGOG*, I GO INTO CONSIDERABLE depth on several of the core issues concerning Islamic Antichrist Theory and why I find fault with it. In this critique, my views are based upon study of various authors who hold the IAT position as well as discussions with colleagues in the eschatology author community, including watching presentations made by many. While I did not have the opportunity to talk directly with Walid Shoebat, I have had the good fortune to spend two hours with Joel Richardson in a polite debate format in which we were able to chat between taping three radio shows for Southwest Radio Church. He is a fine man, full of Christian conviction and with a sincere passion for evangelism and missions. I like Joel very much. Still, while we share an understanding of the gospel's meaning, we disagree on important eschatological issues. These matters mustn't be glossed over.

What (in my humble opinion) is erroneous in the Islamic Antichrist Theory (IAT) remains solely my considered opinion. I know many students of Biblical futurism agree with my position, but there are now many futurists who no longer do.

Much more could be included in this treatise, but for keeping the size of this piece to what fits the *Quick Study Book*™ format, I've limited myself to discuss these ten most crucial points. Therefore, what I identify here are those principal points where IAT fails to acquit itself as the most viable futurist scenario.

## 1. IAT presents a scenario that excludes key scriptures and geopolitical realities. As such, it fails as the best scenario to fit "all the facts".

An Islamic Antichrist, by definition, would rule out other possible candidates for the man of lawlessness. The first and foremost

*Cover of The Islamic Antichrist*

issue is, "What theory best fits the facts as presented in the Bible, as taught throughout Christian history by the most noteworthy futurist scholars, and stands the test of time against geopolitical realities?" Therefore, allow me to summarize the Islamic Antichrist scenario as we begin and then I will move on to discuss a more traditional theory I believe better explains what happens in *the last days,* over the years ahead. I take this tact because, while the IAT ofbut comes from the Middle East, specifically from Turkey, and prophetically is called the "Assyrian" which connotes that he will necessarily be of Middle Eastern

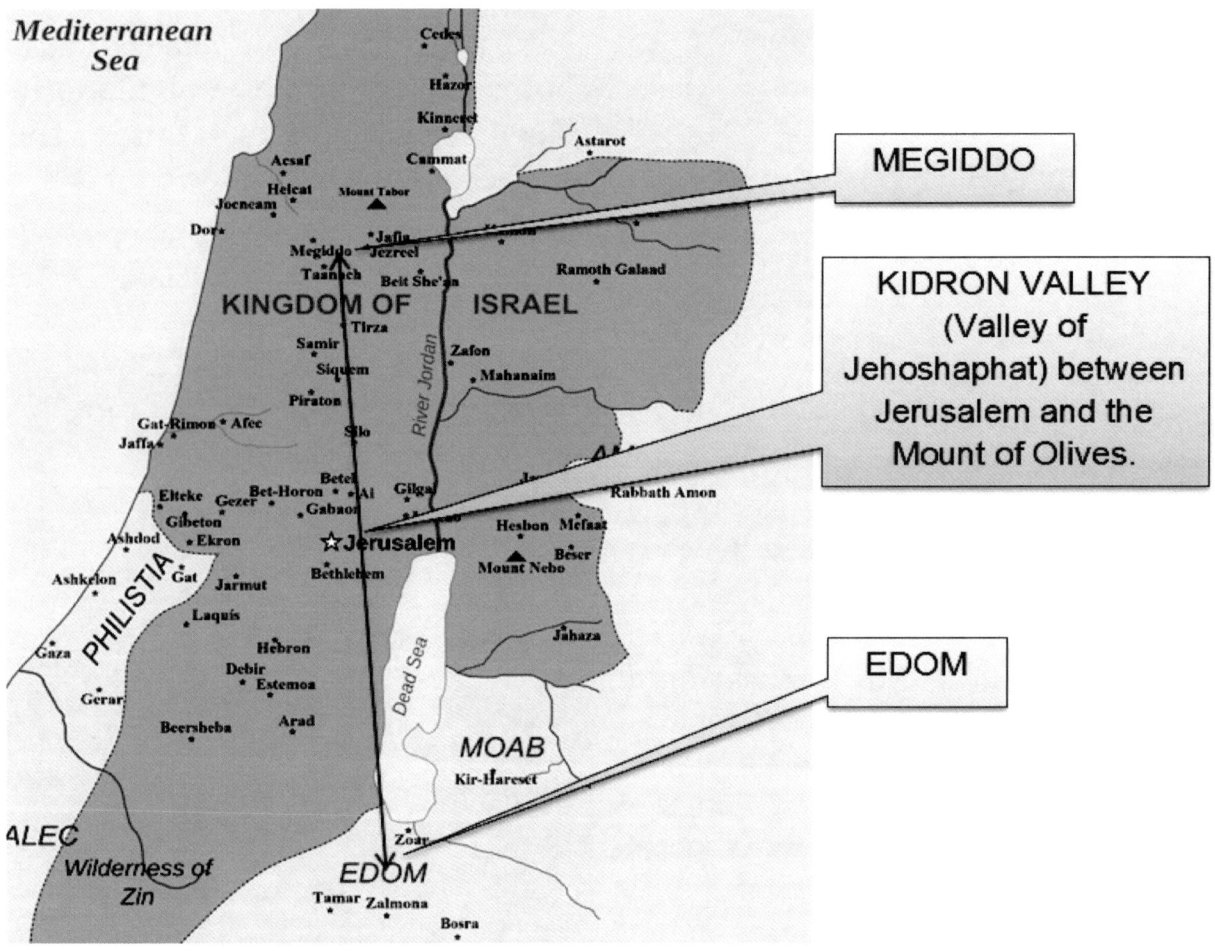

**The Scope of the Battle of Armageddon, from Megiddo to the Valley of Jehoshaphat**

fers a mostly compelling and well-argued position, I believe in a much different scenario as popularized by many peers in the author/researcher community. For convenience in treatment, I will refer to this other view as the "Anglo-American/Luciferian Theory" or **ALT** for convenience, an alternative theory offering a more complete scenario explaining who the "final" Antichrist will be as well as the origin of his power, *both spiritually and geopolitically.*

First to summarize the IAT: The IAT not only asserts the Antichrist will be Muslim, extraction, but not necessarily Jewish.[11]

In contrast, the conventional view proposes that the Antichrist would be a leader of the "revived Roman Empire" – and therefore, presumably a European. Since 1970 (beginning with Hal Lindsey's *Late Great Planet Earth*), Futurism rested upon *the unification of Europe.* But Lindsey made too much of *The Treaty of Rome* (1957) believing that Europe would become the most powerful geo-political confederation on the globe. *Rome has not revived.* His view proved to be untrue, especially so during the past decade. Today, the *Euro* and the European Union both appear on their deathbed.

IAT rightly rejects this view; *but it substitutes an even less likely scenario.* The old Turkish caliphate, the Ottoman Empire, rather than the Roman Empire, *revives* in the last days. Turkey becomes a dominant Middle Eastern power and (apparently) subdues the Shi'ites (Iraq, Iran, and Syria). Thus, IAT assumes *Sunnis prevail over Shia*. (Shoebat asserts the conflict has been mostly mainline media hype). The Islamic Antichrist eventually attacks Israel to eliminate Zionism and kill or disperse Israeli Jews (see below). Later, the Antichrist is defeated in the final battle by Israel's Messiah. However, IAT confuses the personage of Antichrist, his geopolitical powerbase, and the sequence of wars in the end times.

Both theories, the IAT and the ALT, assume the prophecies of the prophet Zechariah are fulfilled in space/time. Zechariah prophesies that the LORD brings salvation to the nation of Israel. While peace does come, Zechariah indicates the process will NOT be painless:

> *Awake, O sword, against my shepherd, and against the man that is my fellow, saith the Lord of hosts: smite the shepherd, and the sheep shall be scattered: and I will turn mine hand upon the little ones.*
>
> *And it shall come to pass, that in all the land, saith the Lord,* **two parts therein shall be cut off and die; but the third shall be left therein.**
>
> **And I will bring the third part through the fire**, *and will refine them as silver is refined, and will try them as gold is tried: they shall call on my name, and I will hear them: I will say, "It is my people": and they shall say, "The Lord is my God".* (Zechariah 13:7-9)

Furthermore, Zechariah indicates that this time of trial will be tumultuous and horrific:

> *Behold, the day of the Lord cometh, and thy spoil shall be divided in the midst of thee. For I will gather all nations against Jerusalem to battle; and the city shall be taken, and the houses rifled, and the women ravished; and half of the city shall go forth into captivity, and the residue of the people shall not be cut off from the city.* (Zechariah 14:1-2)

**Cover, *Apollyon Rising 2012***

The Prophet predicts that plagues will beset those nations that come against Jerusalem:

> *And this shall be the plague wherewith the Lord will smite all the people that have fought against Jerusalem; Their flesh shall consume away while they stand upon their feet, and their eyes shall consume away in their holes, and their tongue shall consume away in their mouth.*
>
> *And it shall come to pass in that day, that a great tumult from the Lord shall be among them; and they shall lay hold every one on the hand of his neighbor, and his hand shall*

> *rise up against the hand of his neighbor.* (Zechariah 14:12-13)

The IAT strongly asserts it will be Turkey that confederates the Islamic nations surrounding Israel, while the ALT asserts it will be Russia who leads the many nations listed in Ezekiel 38-39 which attack Israel.

The IAT contends Islam becomes the one-world religion – but it truly controls only the "world" of the Middle East. All "nations, tongues, and peoples" dominated by the Antichrist are limited to those dwelling in the region, demarcated (if I understand it correctly) by the extent of the old Ottoman Empire (the Middle East, Northern Africa, Eastern Asia, the Balkans, and portions of the Eurasian steppes). *The Antichrist's kingdom is NOT global.* For the most part, the Western Hemisphere is only tangentially involved. Even Europe and Russia appear to play limited roles.

Friend John Price, author of *The End of America* proposes that the Antichrist is a Muslim, but John proposes that the Antichrist obtains power from Europe. John's position constitutes a compromise of sorts built on the conventional view but revised with Islamic elements. Price regards Islam as the final global "one-world religion" held by the conventional view. And John would agree with the IAT regarding how jihad will be made against Israel and that the martyrdom of Christians will be commonplace. But he would disagree with the confluence of Gog with the Antichrist, as well as the wars of Gog/Magog with Armageddon. Additionally, John does not believe that Babylon on the Euphrates will be rebuilt nor would it be the capital of the "Beast Empire" as some propose (Richardson suggests that *Jerusalem* will become the capital of the Antichrist while some conventionalists like Dr. Mark Hitchcock believe Babylon will be rebuilt to be his capital).

I should first point out the conventional view *has undergone considerable development* since the 1970's scenario made popular by Lindsey's *The Late Great Planet Earth* and *The Left Behind* Series of Tim LaHaye and Jerry Jenkins. This has led to the theory I'm labeling the **ALT**. Most no-

Cover, *The Final Babylon*

tably, I find the work of J.R. Church and Gary Stearman to be particularly helpful along with a few others I will mention. Indeed, Church and Stearman opened the door to many advances in Futurist thinking.

In his book, *Daniel's Predicts the Bloodline of the Antichrist,* Church studies the genealogy of the Antichrist from the Book of Daniel and proposes that the Antichrist comprises a person of Greek, Roman, and Jewish ancestry – all three converging into his bloodline. Going back to the Church Fathers who speculated on the origin of the Antichrist, J.R. proposed that the Antichrist would be from the tribe of Dan. *"Dan is a lion's whelp."* (Deuteronomy 33:22) We should recall the Tribe of Dan was associated with the strange goings-on at Mount Hermon, i.e., the Nephilim of Genesis 6 and the Book of Enoch. Dan's tribal ensign originally was "the snake". We should also make note that it was the Canaanites (the Phoenicians) of Tyre and Sidon that dominated the seas for at least one full millennium before the time of Christ. *J.R. assumed Dan was the father of the Danites.* The sea-worthy Danites came to inhabit many of the Greek Isles after leaving their lands in Canaan (refusing to fight the Philistines to possess Danite lands). The person of antiquity to whom J.R. devoted much attention was the heroic *Aeneas* (Virgil's *Aeneid*, his namesake[12]). Aeneas came from the people who would eventually be known as the Spartans, but who fled Troy *after the Trojan War* (and before the Danites became the Spartans) winding up in what is today's Italy, becoming a great grandfather of the (perhaps) mythical twins, Romulus and Remus (Rome being named after Romulus). Thus, Aeneas was Hebrew, Greek, and Roman.

Author Tom Horn in his book, *Apollyon Rising 2012*, also contributed to a more sophisticated perspective, arguing that Antichrist is *the seed of Satan*, incarnated by the principality or power of *Apollyon* or *Abaddon* (the destroyer) from the "bottomless pit" mentioned in Revelation 9. While the Antichrist wasn't revealed in 2012 as Horn intimated he might be, Horn's other assertion was that the U.S.A. comprises a fulfillment of many aspects of the mythic Greek, Roman, and esoteric aspects of the false Messiah, pointing out the many Masonic and Rosicrucian elements in American symbolism (in Washington D.C. in particular), and the tight connection between Freemasonry and Luciferianism that dominates the New Age teachings promulgated by Americans in the twentieth century (Alice Baily, Marilyn Ferguson, and David Spangler). My own books, *POWER QUEST, BOOK ONE: AMERICAN'S OBSESSION WITH THE PARANORMAL* And *POWER QUEST, BOOK TWO: THE ASCENSION OF ANTICHRIST IN AMERICA* took friend Tom Horn's work to an even deeper level, substantiating Tom's theses with considerable additional research. My contention from that point forward: *America plays a crucial part in the last days.* Far from not being mentioned in the Bible, the U.S.A. plays a starring role. Unfortunately, it is not a positive one.

The theory I advanced in these books was built upon an updated conventional view but *switched the identity of the "revived Roman Empire" from the European Union to the U.S. and the U.K.* (think Cecil Rhodes' Anglo-American axis). *THE FINAL BABYLON* (co-authored with Douglas Krieger and Dene McGriff), posited that an American leader could likely become the Antichrist. Thus, the United States would fulfill not only the Old Testament prophecies of the *Daughter of Babylon* but would also incarnate (comprise the final instance of) *Mystery Babylon* (specifically, be "the final Babylon"). In the scenario we offered in 2013, the U.S. would persist deep into the Great Tribulation and not be destroyed by God's judgment (or by the Beast and the 10 kings of Revelation 17) until *late* in Daniel's 70th Week. From my perspective, we did not distinguish the destruction of the *Daughter of Babylon* from *Mystery Babylon's* demise.

While the two "entities" could be the same as we asserted back then, I now believe them to be distinct. Based upon further study, and conferring with friends Price and Benjamin Baruch, and studying Douglas Berner's *The Silence is Broken*, I now believe the United States best fits solely the *Daughter of Babylon* and will be decimated some time before Daniel's 70th week; while *Mystery Babylon* – representing the global gentile system opposing God – will not be consumed entirely by the God's wrath until Antichrist's reign concludes as the age ends.[13]

John the Revelator supplies many details regarding the Beast, the ten kings empowering him, and the harlot they burn with fire:

> *And the beast that was, and is not, even he is the eighth, and is of the seven, and goeth into perdition.*
>
> *And the ten horns which thou sawest are ten kings, which have received no kingdom as yet; but receive power as kings one hour with the beast.*
>
> *These have one mind, and shall give their power and strength unto the beast.*
>
> *These shall make war with the Lamb, and the Lamb shall overcome them: for he is Lord of lords, and King of kings: and they that are with him are called, and chosen, and faithful.*
>
> *And he saith unto me, "The waters which thou sawest, where the whore sitteth*, **are peoples, and multitudes, and nations, and tongues.**
>
> *"And the ten horns which thou sawest upon the beast, these shall hate the whore, and shall make her desolate and naked, and shall eat her flesh, and burn her with fire.*

> *For God hath put in their hearts to fulfill his will, and to agree, and give their kingdom unto the beast, until the words of God shall be fulfilled.*
>
> *And the woman which thou sawest is that great city, which reigneth over the kings of the earth.* (Revelation 17:11-18)

It seems logical to Reconcile *Revelation's harlot* with the *Daughter of Babylon* prophesied against by Old Testament prophets (both are feminine characters). However, the "woman" is also a *city* and Jeremiah's Daughter of Babylon (chapters 50-51) is both *a city* and *a nation* (referred to as Babylon and Chaldea). Additionally, I contend Babylon as a *"city divided into three parts"* (Revelation 16:19), consists of a religious system, an economic power, and a political/military colossus. Thus, all things considered, *Mystery Babylon truly comprises a most profound mystery.*

The scenario put forth in *The Final Babylon*, was based upon considerable research into the reality behind the King of Tyre (Ezekiel 28); the connection of the Phoenicians (i.e., *Canaanites*) to the New World; the identification of the Bible's "Merchants of Tarshish"; the connection of the Queen of Heaven to Ishtar (and Jezebel as an antitype of the harlot of Babylon); and thanks to Krieger, a bit of Old Testament numerology.

My view as elaborated in all three books touching on "America as Babylon" (speaking only for myself, not for Krieger and McGriff) is that the principal religion of the last days *is not Islamic, but* **Luciferian**. The conventional view holds that Satan possesses the Antichrist – whoever this "son of perdition" is. But as Tom Horn argued, in some sense he is literally "the seed of Satan" (other writer researchers today speculate the same, implying some sort of genetic connection!)

The Beast will also be aided by the False Prophet, who welds satanically derived power, despite the superficial appearance as a great leader of the Christian faith (having two horns like a lamb, Rev. 13:8).

In this respect, the Antichrist would fall right in line with the figure of Adolf Hitler whose SS was a knightly order fashioned on the Teutonic Knights amidst the deep occult teachings of Karl Maria Wiligut, Heinrich Himmler's "Rasputin". Furthermore, the Antichrist will rely upon a powerbase that will comprise, at minimum, the elite leaders in the Western World; but more generally "the kings of the earth" (Psalm 2 et al) which is equated with the ten kings of Revelation. It is possible that the so-called *Thirteen Bloodlines of the Illuminati* (as documented by Fritz Springmeier) will be made manifest through this conspiracy. Individuals (whether members of a real Illuminati or not) would be at the heart of The New World Order (NWO), globalism, its manifestation in the United Nations, and even the key financial institutions of the world such as the World Bank, the International Monetary Fund (IMF), and the International Bank of Settlements dominated by the Anglo-American axis. Collectively, this special elite comprises the very heart and soul of the Luciferian conspiracy to establish a one-world government and a Luciferian one-world religion.

The Anglo-American "banksters" (so-called) dominating Wall Street and the City of London, as well as many power players of global corporations, will be mainstays in the power structure of this final installment of the worldwide shadow government. Operating behind the scenes, the elite scions of the Illuminist bloodlines constitute yet another reason why *Mystery Babylon* continues to be so mysterious.

It is my belief and the belief of many other writer-researchers, that these elites are already infused with satanic power activated *ritualistically* to maintain their position and place in the world. Their prominence owes in no small part to unspeakable actions in which they participate. (I speak to this in depth at the conclusion of *Power Quest, Book Two: The Ascendancy of Antichrist in America*).

Today, the United States is the principal incarnation of Mystery Babylon. Its military is the principal enforcer of the NWO. The petrodollar, for the time being at least, remains the one-world currency and facilitates a one-world economy. *The Anglo-American power elite possesses the spirit of Antichrist just as much as darkest elements of the Islamic religion and personages whom Islamic eschatology reveres.*

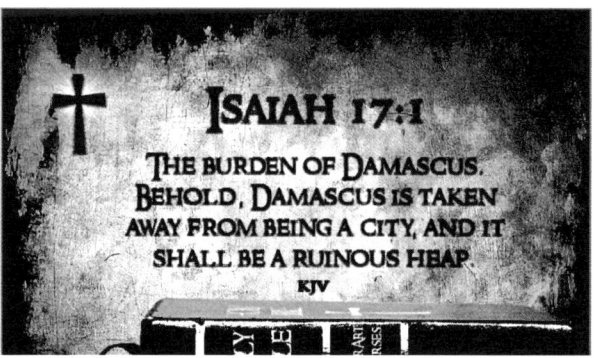

**The Crucial Prophetic Passage of Known as the 'Burden of Damascus'**

However, the power elite of the West *possesses far more power than leaders in the Muslim world*. In many ways, Islam is a religion of the third world, while Luciferianism is the religion of the first world. The best-selling book *The Babylon Code* of Paul McGuire and Troy Anderson (which kindly quotes me on numerous occasions) tends to confirm many of these assertions although the book *does **not** explicitly draw the conclusion that the U.S. or the Anglo-American axis comprises the final incarnation of the Beast system.*

To recap as well as extend this scenario: the U.S. represents the *Daughter of Babylon* described in detail by many of the Bible's prophets, but most specifically by Jeremiah, Isaiah, Obadiah, and Zechariah. It is my view that the United States and Russia (not Turkey) will come to blows at the outset of the War of Gog and Magog, and that this war is the "next great war" in the Middle East (not the now commonly cited war known as the "Psalm 83 War"). As I described in IS RUSSIA DESTINED TO NUKE THE U.S.? as well as the even more recent prequel to this book, *THE NEXT GREAT WAR IN THE MIDDLE EAST,* I speculate (as have many other authors) that Russia will attack and decimate the U.S; but soon afterwards, God Himself will judge Russia (who I believe constitutes Ezekiel's *Gog*) and destroys at least five-sixths of the combined military of Russia and its confederate nations who are predominantly Islamic. (Ezekiel 39:2-4) Unlike the IAT, *I believe the personage of Gog is distinct from the Antichrist and the War of Gog and Magog is distinct from the War of Armageddon* (more about this later).

As stated above, my personal view has progressed to no longer identify the U.S. as the "final" Babylon; rather it is the U.S.A.'s *conflict with Russia* that brings the world to the brink of the Tribulation Period. Post-Ezekiel 39, after the U.S. and Russia are no longer the most dominating powers in the world, it is likely that the Antichrist appears prominently on the scene and becomes the leader to whom all the remaining nations of the world look – to establish the New World Order in an official, formal fashion. He may or may not have a Muslim background. If not a former American leader, he will likely be of royal blood and in my view, likely from Western Europe (England, France, Italy, or even more intriguingly, from Germany).

Hence, the concept of the "revived Roman Empire" of conventional futurist eschatology may ultimately come true, at least in part.[14] Antichrist will consolidate the remaining political, economic, and military power in the world and institute a single monetary system through the so-called "Mark of the Beast". His domination will be substantial but probably not absolute. Powers in Asia (notably China, India, and perhaps Japan) may oppose him to some extent, but ultimately will be influenced to make war against Israel and its Messiah (the "Armageddon Campaign").

The discussion of the Kings of the North, the South, and the so-called third king considered to be Antichrist (the 'Three King Theory' of Daniel 11), constitutes a subject we will take up later.[15] The complexity of that discussion *increases the confusion of Gog with Antichrist*. This may be resolved by discovering that all of Daniel 11 has been fulfilled already – and that there remains no future King of the North, the South, and a third King that appears in Daniel 11. But that is getting ahead of the story.

In summary, I argue that the conventional scenario with the updates suggested here, for the most part reflects a much more widely held view among a majority of leading eschatology scholars today, than does the IAT. From my vantage point, the IAT fails to align all the biblical and geopolitical facts as coherently as the theory I label the Anglo-American/ Luciferian theory (ALT), which is an updated and expanded conventional view.

## 2. Rome destroyed Jerusalem and the Temple (Daniel 9:26-27), whether Syrian conscripts were in the ranks of Rome or not.

IAT believes that the fourth empire talked about by Daniel (in Chapter 7 of Daniel) is a revived Ottoman Empire – not a revived Roman Empire. IAT believes that the colossus of Daniel 2, the colossus who had two legs with feet of iron and clay, represent the conflicted Islamic world split between Shi'ite and Sunni, which "don't mix". Others suppose that if there is a relationship to the Roman Empire, it lies in the fact Rome had both Eastern as well as Western dominions. Chuck Missler provided a study many years ago on this topic (referenced earlier, "The Antichrist: The Alternate Ending" – 2006), asserting that it was indeed possible the revived Roman Empire was the Eastern, not the Western "leg" of the colossus, aka the Roman Empire.

Richardson argues forcibly that the people of the prince to come referenced in Daniel 9:26-27 were *Assyrians* because the Roman Legions at the time the Jewish Temple was destroyed (in 70 A.D.) were garrisoned in the Seleucid region then known as Syria, but in far more ancient times as Assyria.

Chris White, in his stern "debunking" of the Islamic Antichrist Theory, argues that Romans are Romans whether they are Syrians, Jews, or otherwise, since Legionnaires had to be citizens of Rome. He goes even further and contends that at least 90% of these legions were composed of Romans (native to today's Italy). He also points out that while there were a half-dozen different legions involved in the siege at Jerusalem in the first century A.D. (and at least one of which had been garrisoned in Jerusalem for a time), there seems to be little value in stressing the racial or national characteristics of the people of the prince that would "destroy the city and the sanctuary" since most, in his research, were still native Romans and acted under Roman authority. I understand Richardson disputes White's disconfirming facts.

Scholars today, except Islamic Antichrist theorists, continue to assert that the Antichrist will in some sense be of Roman derivation (either racially, culturally, or from a nation dominated by Roman law). Of course, almost all of Western Europe and the Western Hemisphere speak languages that are based on Latin (the so-called *romance languages* – note the connection of **rom**ance to **Rom**e). Even English itself is a blend owing to Latin and Germanic influences. The sculpture and architecture of Washington D.C. is distinctly and intentionally "classical;" i.e., Greco-Roman. Although America is the "New Atlantis" of Francis Bacon, it continues to revere the classical mythology of the Greeks and Romans. *Libertas*, the Roman goddess of Liberty, adorns the top of the Capitol building and also stands as a sentry in New York harbor. The "roman robes" of Lady Liberty verifies her Roman nature.

Many suspect that Libertas is more than just the goddess of liberty, but connects to the "queen of heaven", to Astarte, Ishtar, Venus, and Isis – known also as Europa – who rode the bullish incarnation of Zeus. Europa was, however, *no European* although Europe was her namesake. **Europa** was Tammuz as worshipped in Babylon (the wife/consort of Nimrod according to Alexander Hislop), and the same deity mentioned by Jeremiah. *"The children gather wood, and the fathers kindle the fire, and the women knead their dough, to make cakes to the* **queen of heaven***, and to pour out drink offerings unto other gods, that they may provoke me to anger."* (Jeremiah 7:18, see also 44:17-19, 25). According to Herodotus, she was the goddess worshipped by the Canaanites (aka Phoenicians) 1,000 years before his time when he researched her origins circa 450 B.C. If true, she was the Mother of Heaven of the Phoenicians linked to Baal and the prostitute worship of the Canaanites at Tyre and Sidon. At the time of Christ, the Greco-Roman pantheon continued as the dominant set of gods which symbolized Western *culture and civilization* – such order being the gift of Prometheus, which he stole from Zeus, the lead Olympian.

## 3. Old Testament references to "the Assyrian" as the enemy of Israel don't designate a Syrian Antichrist.

It remains a relatively common position that "The Assyrian" is an appellation for the Antichrist. Exactly why this is so, however, is not completely apparent. We read in Isaiah, *"I will break the Assyrian in My land, And on My mountains tread him underfoot. Then his yoke shall be removed from them, and his burden removed from their shoulders."* (Isaiah 14: 25) But the name may not have anything to do with racial characteristics.

Indeed, there are a series of verses among Old Testament prophets that reference the Assyrian including the use of the name *Asshur* – often translated as a place name instead of a person's name. Citing them for the reader's convenience:

EMBLEM OF ASSHUR.

**Asshur (Nimrod) [Note the empty bow reminiscent of the rider on the white horse depicted in Revelation 6:1-2]**

*Isaiah 10:24-25 - Therefore thus says the Lord GOD of hosts: "O My people, who dwell in Zion, do not be afraid **of the Assyrian**. He shall strike you with a rod and lift up his staff against you, in the manner of Egypt. For yet a very little while and the indignation will cease, as will My anger in their destruction."*

*Isaiah 14:25-26 - That I will break **the Assyrian** in My land, and on My mountains tread him underfoot. Then his yoke shall be removed from them, and his burden removed from their shoulders. This is the purpose that is purposed against the whole earth, and this is the hand that is stretched out over all the nations.*

*Micah 5:3-6 - Therefore He shall give them up, until the time that she who is in labor has given birth; then the remnant of His brethren shall return to the children of Israel. And He shall stand and feed His flock in the strength of the LORD, in the majesty of the name of the LORD His God; and they shall abide, for now He shall be great to the ends of the earth; and this One shall be peace. When **the Assyrian** comes into our land, and when he treads in our palaces, then we will raise against him seven shepherds and eight princely men. They shall waste with the sword the land of Assyria, and the land of Nimrod at its entrances; thus He shall deliver us from **the Assyri-***

***an**, when he comes into our land and when he treads within our borders.*

As I discuss in my previous book (*The Next Great War*), citing friend Peter Goodgame, Asshur is most *likely a reference to Nimrod*. In fact, "The Assyrian" could be nothing more than a symbolic reference employing ancient Assyria as a "generic enemy" of Israel that hailed from Nineveh (a city founded by none other than Nimrod – who also established Babylon).

**Cover, *Islamic Antichrist Debunked***

Nimrod was the first true "type" of antichrist and likely was the antitype of many gods in the pantheon of Egypt and Babylon, then later Greece and Rome. Mythology scholars connect Nimrod with Osiris, Orion, and Apollo. While Apollo was known as the god of music, he was also known as the "Destroyer". This constitutes the meaning behind *Apollyon* and *Abaddon* in the Book of Revelation (Rev. 9:11). Tom Horn addresses this thoroughly in his study of mythology and its influence upon America's founders and Masonic principles in *Apollyon Rising 2012*.

As referenced earlier, the *Book of Micah* makes strong references to the Assyrian. It is in the context of the last days that the venerable John F. Walvoord made this observation regarding the Assyrian:

> One of the prophecies concerning the destruction of Assyria is found in Micah 5:5, 6 where the context seems to indicate a millennial situation. Some expositors have identified "the Assyrian" of Micah 5:5 as the little horn of Daniel 8 and conclude that the future world ruler who will head the Roman Empire will be an Assyrian. This *identification, however, is doubtful*, and it is more probable that Micah, living in the period of Assyria's ascendancy, is merely contrasting here the future glory of Israel with the destruction of Nineveh and of Assyria, which actually took place in the seventh century B.C.[16] [Emphasis mine]

While the appellation "The Assyrian" likely has some reference to the future Antichrist, it should be obvious *The Assyrian* is no reference to his being Muslim. The Islamic Antichrist theory may be playing on today's similar sounding name *Syria* with ancient *Assyria* from which, of course, the name Syria was derived.

While the land area overlaps in part, identifying these two entities would be something of a semantic "play on words". Until the Muslims conquered them in the seventh century A.D., the Assyrians were considered Byzantines (Romans).

Enthrallingly, the Assyrians of today claim that they are *a Christian people* that are now stateless and which suffer persecution (much like the Palestinians). (See the endnote for a detailed discussion from their website.)[17]

To make the point more explicit, the Antichrist could be an American President and still be tagged "The Assyrian" because he represents an enemy to the people of Israel. If he is Muslim, that fact might be entirely coincidental, not necessarily any sort of confirmation that he is the prophesied "AC". In this case, calling him "The Assyrian" would not be literally true – only figuratively so.

Author Chris White also points out that while *Antiochus Ephiphanes IV* was a ruler in Assyria at the time he desolated the Temple (and was clearly an antitype of Antichrist), he was not a Muslim and not a native to Assyria. White points out, "Even the people who want to focus in on Antiochus sometimes overlook the fact that, although he ruled in Syria, *he was a Greek man ruling a Hellenistic empire and worshipping Greek gods*. Calling him a prefiguration of a Muslim ruler would be like calling Julius Caesar a Muslim king because Rome ruled over Egypt."[18] [Emphasis mine]

We must remember that it was Rome that named the region *Palestine* after the destruction of Jerusalem in 135 A.D. (subsequently renamed *Aelia Capitolina*). The Temple mount was plowed and salt sown into the ground at the Temple's location. Jerusalem was scraped away (edifices from the First Temple Period would have been buried deeper underfoot as the Second Temple was built upon the site). Palestine was an unambiguous Roman province, named in part after the Philistines apparently to "rub salt in the wounds" (as well as plowing salt in the grounds!) The Latin Romans protected it for several centuries, and then the Byzantines (the Eastern Romans) occupied the Levant until the Islamic conquest in the *seventh century A.D.*

This symbolic use of an ancient name of peoples in the Bible referencing a future people or person is not without precedent. We see another example of ancient names referencing future foes, the most relevant being *Edom* and the *Edomites*. This instance is especially germane to my point.

Edom was the regional area centered on the city of Petra and Mount Seir (lying between the Dead Sea and the Gulf of Aqaba). **Esau** established the city only 300 to 400 years *after* Noah's flood. For centuries Edom was one of the greatest kingdoms on earth and stood as a mortal enemy to the Jews. This area, and the city of Petra its capital, actually comprised the third most mentioned city in the Bible. However, Edom was abandoned for a time (before Christ) and its people moved to the west and lived south of Jerusalem. They became known as the *Idumeans*. In fact, King Herod was an Idumean, not a Jew, and as such was regarded as the descendant of Esau. No surprise then that the Jews chaffed under his rule.

We should make a special note that Jewish scholars came to identify Edom symbolically as Rome. Gary Stearman offers a compelling argument that many Jewish scholars frequently reference Edom as a name for Rome, connecting both Edom and Rome symbolically as Israel's enemy "in *Messianic* times."[19] Stearman quotes *Rabbi Ibn Ezra Radak*, "I love the Romans because the Torah commands, 'You shall not despise the Edomite, for he is your brother.'" (Deuteronomy 23:8) [20] "The Assyrian" is similar.

## 4. IAT wrongly argues the empire of Antichrist has only a regional, not global span of control.

Islamic Antichrist Theory sees the scope of the Bible's last days' prophecy as a regional, *not a global phenomenon*. This position is pegged on the somewhat common, but in my view academic cliché, that "the Bible is a Jewish, Mediterranean book" (presupposing Jewish concepts and Greek ones are highly incompatible). Therefore, it's as if the Bible only professes truths obvious to people in a geographical area running about 1,000 miles in all directions (a radius extending) from Jerusalem. This topic deserves a study on its own to counter *the overemphasis upon Jewish "roots" in our day* with its disdain if not downright antagonism toward Christian traditions, some creeds, and all Christian holidays over against Jewish holy days. I will but barely touch on my reaction here.

IAT justifies its *parochial* perspective on several undeniable facts: the Bible was (1) penned almost exclusively by Jews, (2) pertains to the history of the Jews, and (3) considers Jerusalem to be the center of the world. But do these facts demand that we interpret biblical eschatology only from the standpoint of Jews living in the time of Christ, of even earlier, in the time of the Prophets? If so, should we also understand the Gospel only from the standpoint of the Jews? If you answer affirmatively, I would like to call the Apostle Paul to the witness stand. He might have a different viewpoint. But since Paul no longer resides with us, we must obtain his opinion from his writings, to put "Jewishness" in proper perspective:

> *For ye have heard of my conversation in time past in the Jews' religion, how that beyond measure I persecuted the church of God, and wasted it: And profited in the Jews' religion above many my equals in mine own nation, being more exceedingly zealous of the traditions of my fathers. (Galatians 1:13-14)*

> *There is neither Jew nor Greek, there is neither bond nor free, there is neither male nor female: for ye are all one in Christ Jesus. And if ye be Christ's, then are ye Abraham's seed, and heirs according to the promise. (Galatians 3:28-29)*

"Having a Jewish mindset" does not sanction conceptions or ideas that conflict with the revelation given to the Church and written in Koine Greek; just as "thinking like a Greek" does not overturn the plain teaching of the Law or the Prophets written in Hebrew. Neither should we judge one's interpretation of Bible prophecy out of bounds because it lies beyond Israel's borders.

The Hebrews regarded their principal enemy literally and symbolically to be *Babylon* on the Euphrates, which existed less than one thousand miles from Jerusalem. But distance had nothing to do with the disparity. Likewise, the Jews' enemies today (about whom the Bible prophesies) live alongside and halfway around the world. *The relevant issue consists in their hatred for Israel's existence and challenge to God's plan for His people.*

Bible Prophecy knows no distance. *The four empires of Daniel 2 and 7 were those that had dominion over Israel, concurrent with or just after the time of Daniel and Ezekiel.* Empires outside of the region are of no concern only because they had no influence on Israel. Indeed, it is quite true that the list of Empires in Revelation 17 includes a list of seven empires, (plus the eighth, the Antichrist who is really just one of the seven) which are those that have in the past or in the future directly dominated (of will dominate) the Jews.

The Ottoman Empire never had any influence on the Jewish nation. When it reigned, the Jews were "not at home." That was not true for the other empires Daniel mentions. *Even more should this principle hold true for the existing empire when Jesus was on the earth.* If we dismiss Rome, the empire ruling over Judea when Jesus lived there,

*And the beast that was, and is not, even he is the eighth, and is of the seven, and goeth into perdition.*

*And the ten horns which thou sawest are ten kings, which have received no kingdom as yet; but receive power as kings one hour with the beast.*

**Plaque from Mamertine Prison where Paul was beheaded in Rome**

and replace it with an empire that had no influence over the Jewish nation, of what relevance is that to Bible prophecy? I would argue, rather adamantly in fact: it would have *no relevance at all*.

We read of these seven (eight) empires:

*And here is the mind which hath wisdom. The seven heads are seven mountains, on which the woman sitteth.*

*And there are seven kings: five are fallen, and one is, and the other is not yet come; and when he cometh, he must continue a short space.*

*These have one mind, and shall give their power and strength unto the beast.* (Revelation 17:9-13)

IAT theorists reject Rome as one of the four empires Daniel mentions to make room for the Ottoman Empire to be included as the fourth empire in his vision. From a hermeneutical standpoint, this requires some exegetical gymnastics since IAT theorists assert Daniel doesn't intend Rome to be his fourth empire; and yet John does include Rome in his list of seven (eight) empires (number six, the one that "is" following after the five that have fallen). This then leaves another empire yet to arise, i.e., *the seventh*. And the eighth is Antichrist. Yet John tells us the Antichrist is really either one of the seven or is composed in part from all seven empires. If true, the question is *why Daniel would leave Rome out*. From my perspective, the response from IAT seems somewhat contrived.

IAT argues that Daniel's fourth beast was the Ottoman Empire, primarily because that Empire had a larger area of control than any of the other empires Daniel mentions. From their viewpoint, because Islam was more spread out at its peak across greater landmass, IAT says this constitutes what was meant by Daniel saying, it "crushes all the others". That is, however, not necessarily so obvious to readers that approach the argument "in neutral" or without an old atlas handy.

IAT also suggests that the Muslims deserve to replace Rome because *Muslims are much meaner than the Romans ever were*. We know that Rome beheaded its enemies as well as crucifying them – crucifixion being the cruelest form of death as it lasts for days – especially compared to beheading which lasts but a few seconds. Being a citizen of Rome, Paul was beheaded (perhaps along with dozens of the Praetorian Guard whom he converted to the faith while in the ancient Roman Mamertine Prison[21]). Arguing who is crueler between ancient Rome and current-day jihadists, amounts to a debate that neither deserves to win. Methinks it all depends on whether the one who judges personally experienced both forms of death in order to make a fair comparison. That being impossible, it's best to condemn them both as "cruel and unusual" as befits Americans.

It is true that in land area, the Ottoman Empire exceeded the empire of the (1) Medes and Persians, (2) the Greek Empire of Alexander and his four successors, and (2) the Roman Empire. Of course, I would point out that the "Greco-Roman Empire" could be distinguished (from a cultural perspective) as longer lasting while the Holy Roman Empire could be argued as greater since it had both political and religious components (both priests and kings) which lasted 1,000 years plus eight, from the coronation of Charlemagne in 800 A.D. until Napoleon's defeat in 1808. And the effects of the latter two, in many respects, has held sway globally more than any of the other empires (including the Ottoman). Here I am speaking in terms of architectures, laws, and customs as standards for almost the entire world, not just Western Europe and the United States.

So is Islamic Antichrist Theory right to interpret Daniel's fourth empire as the Ottoman Empire and leaving the Roman Empire completely out of the picture? Hardly.

This appears NOT to be one of the stronger arguments for IAT especially if one also considers that the Ottoman Empire did not really catch hold until the fifteenth century; Constantinople (Istanbul) was not conquered until 1453; and the Ottoman Empire was in tatters by the middle of the nineteenth century. (If my logic still seems lacking, I cover more about the weakness of the Ottoman Empire "argument" in the prequel to this book.)

## 5. Saudi Arabia (and Mecca) are mistakenly regarded as Mystery Babylon in Islamic Antichrist Theory.

Walid Shoebat has been vocal on this assertion; Joel Richardson appears to be less so. But since they collaborated on Shoebat's breakout book and their concepts are usually considered together, we should assume Richardson accepts the premise that "Mystery Babylon is Saudi Arabia" until he publicly disavows it.[22] As we will see, this argument may be the weakest aspect of the IAT. Thus, there is a reason to suspect that Joel Richardson, (who is most circumspect in his writings and lectures), might not emphasize this tenet of the IAT.

According to Shoebat, Saudi Arabia is the "harlot of Revelation" that rides the Beast – and this Beast is Turkey. We will deal more with the possibility that Turkey is "the Beast" in a moment. But first, let's turn to Mecca and Saudi Arabia as the fulfillment of "Mystery Babylon'. Does the Bible's testimony justify this identification?

In the last section, I used the metaphorical language "exegetical gymnastics". If that was true for reconciling the empires mentioned by Daniel and John (leaving Rome out of Daniel's four empires but including it in John's eight), then the assertion that Saudi Arabia fulfills the prophecy of Mystery Babylon requires exegetical *acrobatics*.

Chris White chides Shoebat on this score:

> "Shoebat's method of interpreting these prophecies is extremely unorthodox, and while that is not always a bad thing, it should be noted that very few people, if any, in the history of the church would apply the methods of interpretation that he does."[23]

I suppose that sometimes being a "man without peers" can be a bad thing.

Shoebat's argument builds upon Isaiah 21, *"The Burden of Dumah"*, which mentions a number of cities just north of Arabia and other cities in northern Saudi Arabia of today. White quotes Shoebat from his (and Richardson's) book, *God's War on Terror*:

> Some might argue that the context of Isaiah 21 is only historical. But it is difficult to ignore the multiple references throughout the Book of Isaiah to Kedar, Tema, Dedan and *Dumah*. Dumah is in Saudi Arabia near Yathrib (Medina), and today is known as "Dumat el-Jandal." [Says Shoebat] "Contenders to this interpretation would have a difficult time refuting the very direct Biblical references. The names used in these passages make it clear that the reference is not to Rome or literal Babylon on the Euphrates River. Not once do they speak of Rome, Nineveh, Ur, Babel, Erech, Accad, Sumer, Assur, Calneh, Mari, Karana, Ellpi, Eridu, Kish, or Tikrit. All of these literal locations are in Arabia, which was part of the ancient Babylonian Empire.[24]

Of course, Shoebat is contrasting Saudi Arabia and Mecca with Iraq and historical Babylon, and not a Western country like the U.S. and a city like New York City. When objectively considering the prophecies in Isaiah, Jeremiah, and Obadiah and considering how its prophecies might be fulfilled in the world today, Mecca never comes to mind, but New York City fits the bill very well. Having covered this already extensively in *The Final Babylon* and in *Is Russia Destined to Nuke the U.S.?* I will avoid digressing here to recite the many prophecies directed toward the United States and New York.

From White's viewpoint, he challenges that the cities listed by Shoebat (although they may refer accurately to cities in or near Saudi Arabia), automatically demands the conclusion that Isaiah was predicting a future *Mystery Babylon* there since *the prophecy in Isaiah had already been fulfilled in Isaiah's day.* Specifically, the prophecy was realized during the reign of King Hezekiah, who unwisely (against the counsel of God's prophet Isaiah), joined a rebellion led by an unfortunate rebel, Merodach-Baladan, who took control of the then city of Babylon (it was destroyed and rebuilt afterwards) and came against the *Assyrian Empire* (100 years before the day of Nebuchadnezzar and Daniel, who lived in the seventh century B.C.). This deepened hostilities between Israel and Assyria, which would eventually culminate in the destruction of Israel – the northern Kingdom – with its peoples soon scattered to the four winds. White summarizes the prophecy and its fulfillment with some fascinating historical details unlikely to be familiar to most readers:

> The battle, when it finally came, was devastating for the rebel alliance. The Assyrian king, Sennacherib, who by this time was totally fed up with all the trouble that the city of Babylon was causing Assyria, completely destroyed the city. The complete destruction of Babylon and its temples, down to the foundations, is attested to in the historical inscriptions of the time as well as by modern archeologists. The destruction of Babylon shocked the world, mainly because temples in the city, which were considered very holy by many in the area, were also destroyed. Later when Sennacherib's sons assassinated him, they seemed to suggest it was in retaliation for his completely destroying Babylon and its temples. Eight years later, the Assyrians began rebuilding the city from scratch. This marks the only time in history that the city of Babylon was completely destroyed. [25]

White proceeds to dismantle the relevance of the cities mentioned in Isaiah as they play into the historical account of this rebellion. He also asserts there is no obvious reason to suspect that Isaiah 21 has a "double fulfillment" (whose second fulfillment would take place in the last days) and even less reason to speculate that Saudi Arabia is the best candidate to fulfill the prophecies of "Mystery Babylon" since the only reasons would seem to be (1) Mecca is a city in Saudi Arabia; (2) Mecca is a city where Islam is centered, a religion that is avowedly anti-Christian. Shoebat's argument is, in effect, circular. If we assumed that Buddhism was the religion of Antichrist, then it would be just as smart to point to the area of Lumbini in the Shakya republic of Nepal and declare it "Mystery Babylon" if the Bible had mentioned one or two of its towns, since the Buddha was born there (according to Buddhist tradition).

Furthermore, I would make the point that Islam constitutes a rather obvious variant of Christianity, replacing Jesus as the central figure, affirming that God is one, and that Mohammed's Quran and his sayings (the hadiths) simply replace the New Testament. There is no mystery here at all. Mecca is well known and it is quite well established that it opposes the God of the Bible and His son, Jesus Christ. On the other hand, the identification of *Mystery Babylon* is NOT obvious. Babylon represents many heresies and different instances of opposition to God across the globe and since time immemorial.

Unlike Mystery Babylon in Revelation (a city that Revelation says – without any explanation – divides into three parts), Mecca possesses only a religious element – it has neither *political power* nor *economic hegemony*. In GDP, Saudi Arabia ranks no better than thirteenth in the world. Saudi Arabia is important economically because it has supported the Petrodollar within OPEC, insisting it remains the only way oil can be bought and sold. Thus, our world currency is based on oil (note: a vital but not unique commodity produced in Saudi Arabia as well as in the U.S., which produces near equal amounts). But this does not make Saudi Arabia a global economic power comparable to the Anglo-American alliance of *Wall Street and the City of London*. Compared to the U.S./U.K., Saudi Arabia pales in comparison. The United States stands apart as the world's hegemon in economics, politics, military power, cultural influence, and even religious influence.

**Cover, *The Babylon Code***

Many teachers counsel that we should think of Mystery Babylon, first and foremost, as a global "system" opposed to God, and not one city, nation, or religion in particular. Troy Anderson and Paul McGuire advance this thesis in their latest offering, *The Babylon Code*. However, Revelation's references seem to indicate that while it is more than one city and one nation, there may well be one city and one nation in particular that, as an icon, *represents the system as a whole*. It is my view that we aren't dealing with an "either/or" situation. Mystery Babylon has a multi-faceted nature: it presents a *concept* of occult worship and it stands as a *symbol* against biblical religion and the God of the Bible. But it is also *incarnated* in a city and nation. Just as Jerusalem and Israel are icons of the Holy City and the People of God, they also exist geographically and politically. Mystery Babylon incarnates the evil of ancient Babylon and promotes its "wares" worldwide, dominating in virtually every classification of power that matters: as mentioned before, it ranks out first in political, economic, military, and cultural categories. But does it dominate religiously too? Historicists argue that Roman Catholicism is clearly Mystery Babylon. I disagree. I argue that America has almost as much impact in spiritual matters as does the Roman Catholic Church. When one considers America's obsession with the paranormal, the New Age Movement and its teachings, Luciferianism, and explicit Satanism it remains a difficult task to find a city or a nation that surpasses it.

The U.S. initiated *transhumanism* with the eugenics movement (which the Germans learned from us) beginning at the turn of the twentieth century. This notion of improving humanity and transcending our limitations constitutes a religion in many ways (which I won't delve into here). Slightly before that, in the 1890s, Buddhism was virtually dead until Henry Steel Olcott rekindled it working in tandem with

Madame Helena Petrovna Blavatsky when the Theosophical Society of America was founded in New York City. The U.S. continues to export perhaps the world's most evangelistic religion growing at the fastest rate of any religion: Mormonism, founded by Joseph Smith in the 1830s on principles borrowed from the occult and Freemasonry. More generally, occultism blossomed especially well throughout New England and New York from the 1820s until the 1920s. Luciferianism was at the base of Lucis Trust (founded by Alice Ann Bailey and her husband Foster Bailey) still associated with the United Nations. The New World Order is more than a catchphrase, centered in New York City with such institutions as the Council on Foreign Relations and unofficially manifested in the United Nations. Indeed, it was America's elite that has attempted to conjure world peace for almost a century, beginning after the First World War with the League of Nations, then after the Second World War with the U.N., and finally as the Leader of the Free World to create "ex officio" global government through the NWO, constructing the economic means to do so with the International Monetary Fund, the World Bank, and the International Bank of Settlements. The United States of America has created and cultivated what constitutes the most dominating form of secular humanism the world has ever known.

Yes, in religion too, the United States has supplied the world its most relevant and compelling spiritual enterprise for the wealthy elite and power players throughout the world. In all of these respects, the United States stands without equal.

While most Christians assume that America was founded a "Christian Nation", this is debatable as most of the nation's founders were Freemasons and deists. Consumerism and corporatism drive most of our top politicians, corporate leaders, and entertainers, serving as the underlying basis for what we could now call "this godless endeavor". (See this author's in depth study: *Power Quest, Book One: America's Obsession with the Paranormal*, to understand why America's religious affections are the essential stuff of Mystery Babylon.)

## 6. Turkey is mistakenly identified as the powerbase of the Antichrist.

The cornerstone of IAT is the belief that Turkey will become the great power of the last days and will be the nemesis of Israel. The Beast's power will be built by Turkish military and economic capability. Joel Richardson points out that many Imams predict Turkey will lead Islam once again right before the Mahdi appears. Of course, as I would hastily point out, just because Muslim scholars cite Islamic prophecy as proof texts, doesn't mean that these prophecies will necessarily come to pass.

As stated earlier, the traditional teaching of a "mortal head wound healed" and a resurrection of Antichrist, for IAT theorists, means that the Ottoman Empire will come back to life – it will be revived. As I point out in *The Next Great War in the Middle East*, many other writers following the lead of Shoebat and Richardson, contend that Recep Tayyip Erdoğan, Turkey's president, seeks to make Turkey a caliphate with himself at its center.

When the Ottoman Empire ended in 1924, it sought to modernize and become more

"Western" – following the lead of the English and the French. However, beginning about a decade ago, Turkey reversed this near century-long trend, moving back to more traditional Islamic values, shunning many Western customs and culture. Today, Erdoğan seeks to reinstate fundamentalist Islamic values in his country as well as a government constituting a true caliphate.

**President, Recep Tayyip Erdoğan**

Geopolitically, Turkey is a real presence in the Middle East. It continues to have a strong and strategic link to the West, as it remains a NATO member. At the current time, Erdoğan seeks to improve relations with Israel even while he seeks to forcibly remove Bashar al' Assad, Syria's president. As mentioned before, Turkey, being Sunni, has teamed with the other major Sunni power in the region, Saudi Arabia, to support rebel forces in Syria with money and equipment (ISIS and Jabhat al-Nusra, the Al-Qaeda affiliate in Syria). This has put Turkey at odds with Russia who has pledged support to Assad and who bombed the dickens out of these rebel groups.[26]

In late November 2015, Turkey downed a Russian fighter-bomber and killed a Russian pilot. This nearly led to a war between Russia and Turkey. The rebellion against Assad stands at a crisis point with many of the remaining functional rebel groups (led by ISIS and Al-Nusra) holed up in Aleppo, northern Syria. In March 2016, a cease-fire was enacted between the U.S.-led coalition, Russia, and *97 distinct rebel groups* in Syria; but attacks on ISIS and Al-Nusra were still permitted by the terms of the cease-fire. Whether this situation finally provokes war, or even more frightening ignites World War III, at this time remains anyone's guess.

However, I have been steadfast in my insistence that Russia will continue its support of the Shi'ite leaders in Syria, Iraq, and Iran – standing against the Sunni alliance of Turkey, Jordan, Saudi Arabia, and to a lesser extent Egypt. (Hezbollah controls Lebanon that comprises an Iranian Shia proxy). Recall that the U.S. left a power vacuum in the region when it removed its troops in 2010-2011, which Russia was only too happy to fill. Over the past half-decade, Russia has become a player again in the Middle East; while the U.S. much less so. Unlike the U.S., Russia will not relinquish the inroads made within the region. Russia has been "hooked" into the conflict between Shia and Sunni (a reference to Ezekiel 38, the conflict being the *hook*) and will likely remain in Syria indefinitely with a growing presence, leading up to "the next great war" which I argue is the War of Gog and Magog.

While some argue that Ankara, Turkey exists "directly north" of Jerusalem (and

Moscow isn't), Damascus also sits due north and resides even closer to Israel. Russian military equipment placed in Syria only makes Russia more likely to be Gog.

war develop, however, between Turkey and Russia, NATO will not necessarily be drawn into the conflict, as Turkey appears to have been the aggressor. Additionally,

**Russian Jets Bomb ISIS Oil Tanker Trucks Crossing the Turkish Border**

Where does this leave Erdoğan and Turkey? Erdoğan has been accused of supporting ISIS outright and facilitating truckloads of ISIS oil crossing its borders for sale, enriching ISIS to the tune of millions of dollars in revenues every week. Meanwhile, the United States appears to have been caught with its hand in the cookie-jar, covertly supporting ISIS and Jabhat al-Nusra (along with Turkey), with military weapons and training with virtually nothing to show for its efforts after two billion dollars expended. Additionally, the whole Benghazi affair of 2012 has been linked to CIA gun running, moving weapons from the cache of the late dictator Muammar Gadhafi, through Turkey to the Syrian rebels. As it now stands, should

the Turkish government continues to shell the Kurds incessantly, despite the Kurds being America's best ally in the region. Turkey regards the Kurds as a rebel force, while the Kurds see themselves seeking to win back lands taken from them over the past century. They remain committed to undermining Turkish sovereignty.

Given this tangled mess, could Turkey possibly sever its ties with NATO? Will they join with Russia?

Prophecy teachers often say this *must* happen, since Russia is deemed the leader of the alliance of Muslim nations against Israel (i.e., Ezekiel 38-39). Indeed, the alliance of nations in Ezekiel's list appears to include Turkey (Meschech, Tubal, Gomer) as well as Iran (Persia) despite the fact that Turkey and Iran are enemies in our present day.

From our current vantage point, this comprises the unresolved geopolitical and prophetic puzzle. If one conjectures that the War of Gog and Magog happens after the Millennium (a thousand years from now!) – the position that Chris White, scholar Michael Heiser, and a few other eschatology writers take – it becomes a non-issue.  Obviously then, something must change in the alliance structures of the current belligerents.  Perhaps it will be a war altering the balance of power, or even a nuclear exchange of tactical nuclear weapons.

But the present-day alignment does not allow for Turkey leading the Shia (meaning Iran, Iraq, and Syria).  It has been my opinion (speculation based upon my interpretation of Bible prophecy), that Turkey, far from leading the invasion against Israel prophesied in Ezekiel 38, may not participate at all – being intimated by Russia and feeling that it does not have backing by NATO.  Instead, Russia will occupy Syria with a new puppet leader placed in charge (Assad will not be president much longer). Russia then dominates the "Shia Crescent" (as it has become known, referring to the land surrounding the Tigris and Euphrates Rivers, running from Damascus to Baghdad – see the map above).

To be more precise, I speculate that Russia will support an Iranian attack on (Sunni) Saudi Arabia to wrest control of Mecca and Medina from the Sunnis (on behalf of the Shi'ites).  Iran attacks just after Russia attacks the United States (and possibly London) with nuclear weapons, to neutralize the United States and the United Kingdom in a gambit to wrest control of all the

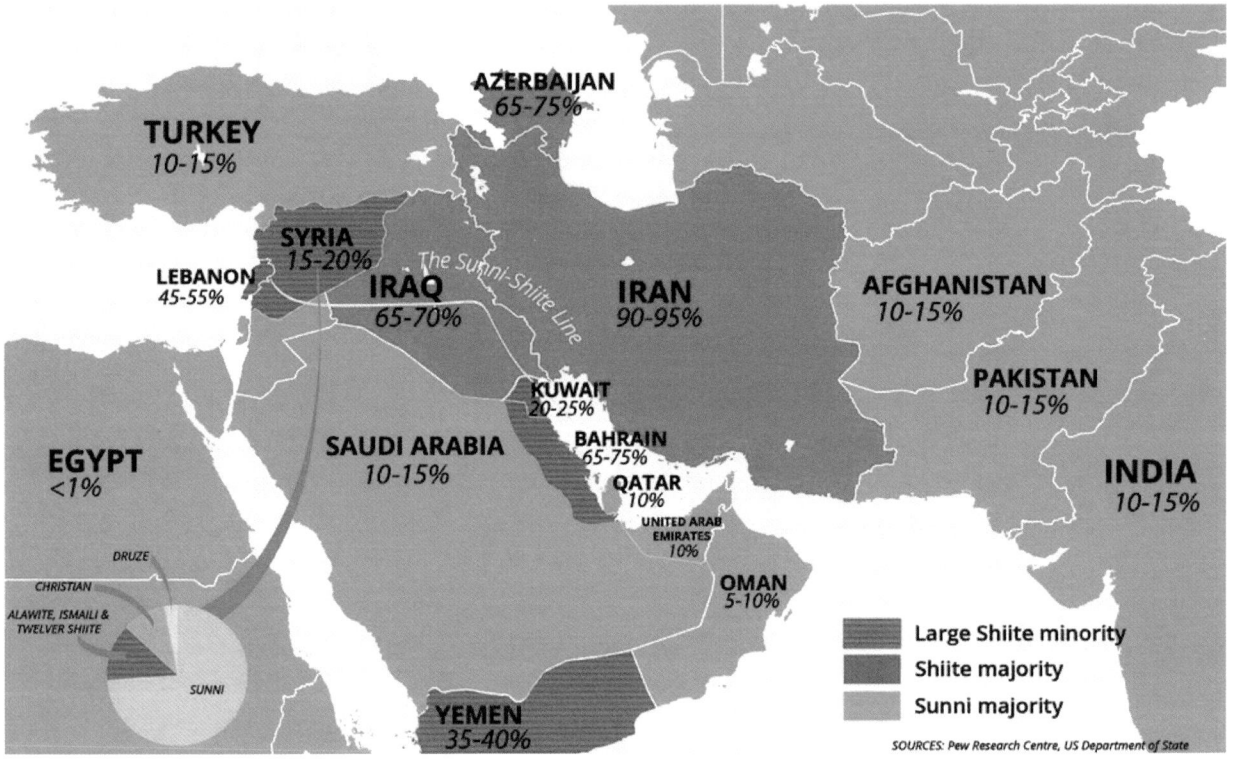

**Shia as Percent of Total Muslim Population by Islamic Country**

oil in the Middle East – directly or indirectly – along with its Shia allies. From Russia's position, this would necessarily achieve a complete "reversal of fortune" ruining the economies of the West and placing itself in the driver's seat. Such a bold move would free Russia of a half-trillion in debt to Western bankers. What this would also mean is that Russia corners the market on oil by taking Saudi oil and the oil recently discovered in the Golan Heights (in the disputed territory of Israel claimed by Syria.) 27 Why would Putin (or a successor) go to this extreme? Russia grows increasingly desperate as the ruble crumbles, the price of oil remains below $50/barrel, and Russia's dream of reinstating its Empire teeters on the brink. The status quo soon will change – otherwise Russia fragments.

## 7. Meschech, Tubal, Gomer, and Beth-Togarmah: not just names for ancient Anatolia (Turkey)

Another core component of the IAT is that the tribal names listed in Ezekiel 38 – that stem from the so-called 'Table of Nations' in Genesis 10 – comprise the alliance of Gog and Magog that conspires to attack Israel. These names reference the sons and grandsons of Japheth, the son of Noah (father of all Caucasians including the Indo-European peoples).

> *Son of man, set your face toward Gog of the land of Magog, the prince of Rosh, Meshech, and Tubal, and prophesy against him and say, 'Thus says the Lord God "Behold, I am against you, O Gog, prince of Rosh, Meshech and Tubal. I will turn you about and put hooks into your jaws, and I will bring you out, and all your army, horses and horsemen, all of them splendidly attired, a great company with buckler and shield, all of them wielding swords: Persia, Ethiopia, and Put with them, all of them with shield and helmet; Gomer with all its troops, Beth-Togarmah from the remote parts of the north will all its troops – many peoples with you.* (Ezekiel 3: 1-6, NASV)

I won't delve into all aspects of this issue here as I spend a full chapter in my previous book clarifying the sons of Japheth and the many peoples from his ancestral line, along with the location of their settlements throughout Eurasia and beyond to the remotest parts of the earth. That data cannot be easily summarized in a few words. Suffice it to say that the key argument made by Richardson is this: each name in Ezekiel's list refers to peoples settled soon after the flood of Noah in the area we call *Anatolia* (today's Turkey); and that virtually any old atlas one can obtain (and Richardson has many) will substantiate the fact that these tribes originated in Anatolia and lived between and south of the Black and Caspian Seas.

Richardson has commented on this matter extensively, including a recent article written and published on-line at *Prophezine*. 28 In his article, he cites just a few of these atlases from which he presents maps of the area along with the following commentary:

- The Oxford Bible Atlas says of Meshech and Tubal that they are, "regions in Asia Minor [Turkey]."

- Old Testament scholar Daniel I. Block, in the New International Commentary on Ezekiel, says, "It seems best to interpret Magog as a contraction of an original māt Gūgi, 'land of Gog,' and to see here a reference to the territory of Lydia in western Anatolia [Turkey]."

- The Zondervan Illustrated Bible Dictionary states, "Magog, possibly meaning 'the land of Gog,' was no doubt in Asia Minor [Turkey] and may refer to Lydia."

- The IVP Bible Background Commentary lists Magog, Meshech, Tubal, and Togarmah as "sections or peoples in Asia Minor" [Turkey].
- The New Unger's Bible Dictionary, under the entry for "Magog," states, "It is clear that Lydia [Turkey] is meant, and that by 'Magog,' we must understand, 'the land of Gog.'"

this region, until Ezekiel talks about Magog, Meschech, Tubal, Gomer, and Beth-Togarmah. What is striking: by looking beyond his sons to Japheth's grandsons, we already see that significant dispersion had happened, as their names gave rise to place names throughout Eurasia before

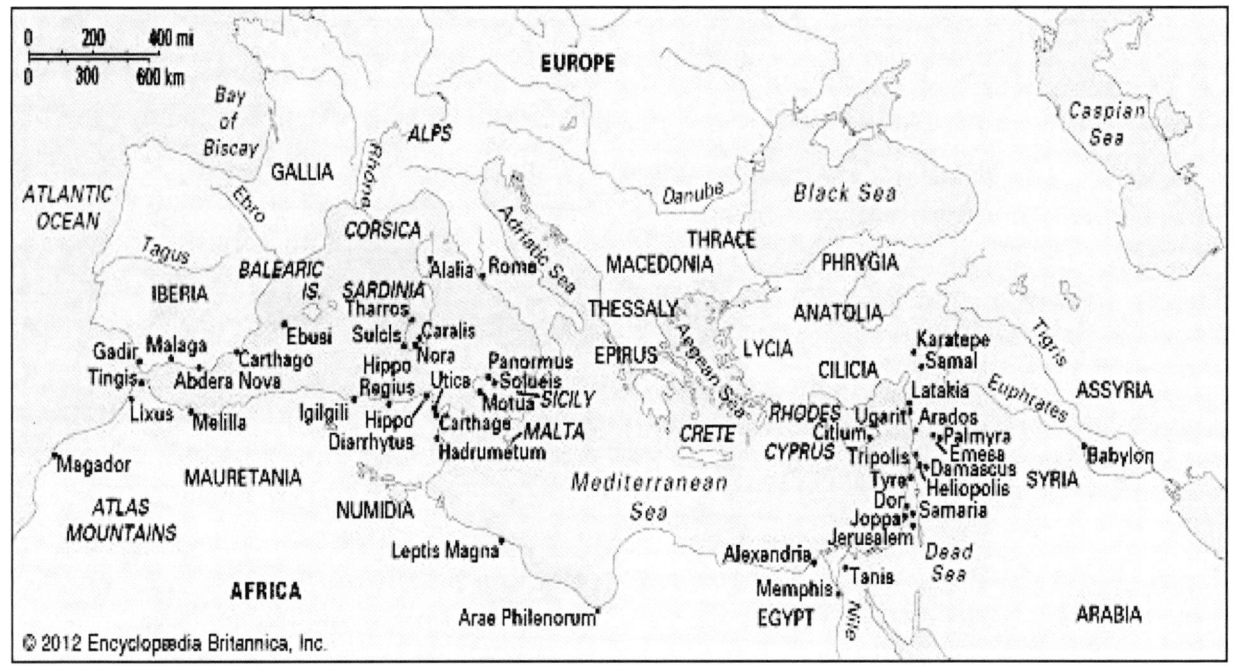

**The Mediterranean at the time of Phoenician Empire (Circa 550 B.C.)**
**©Encyclopedia Britannica**

I would certainly stipulate that the original dwelling place for Japheth's sons, Magog, Gomer, Tubal, and Meschech is most certainly Anatolia. But that may not be saying much. The issue is whether it matters that the sons of Japheth, these four sons (there were seven altogether), and the first two or three generations thereafter (settling down in the region as many of their families no doubt did after the Flood), *remained **only** there,* never migrating anywhere else between that time and almost *two millenniums later* when Ezekiel was prophesying about the great war in the days leading up to the coming of Messiah. It other words, it was almost 1,800 years from the time of Japheth's lineage settling in and around Ezekiel's day. Consequently, it leads me to ask, "When do you draw the line and say, "The peoples spoken of by Ezekiel refer only to the original dwelling place of the peoples and not subsequent generations that migrated across (perhaps) the entire Northern Hemisphere?"

I argue any such "line drawing" is arbitrary.

Most demographers would indicate that by the time of Ezekiel, about 2,000 years from Noah's flood, the world was populated in all its parts. The three sons of Noah – Ham, Shem, and Japheth – did exactly what God had commanded – they were *fruitful, multiplied and replenished the earth.*

The question seems to be: "When Ezekiel speaks of Meschech, Tubal, Gomer, Beth-Togarmah, etc., is he referring to large peo-

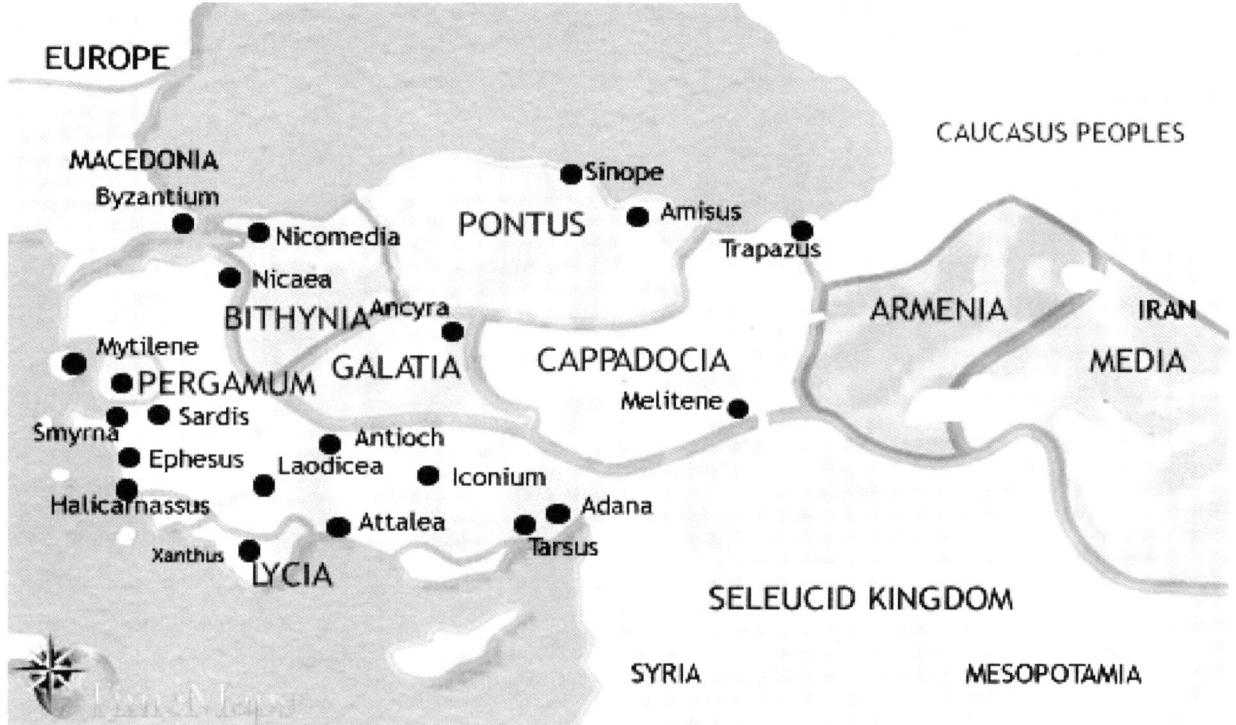

Map of Anatolia during the Seleucid Kingdom (circa 150-100 B.C.) © Time Maps

ple groups and where their multitudes would ultimately inhabit, or just the areas where they settled originally soon after the Flood?" As Richardson rightly says, many maps show the area of Anatolia as the home to these tribes as identified in the table of nations (Genesis 10). But does that disclose *where they were located in Ezekiel's time?* Or perhaps more relevantly, *where they will be located in the last days?*

When doing this analysis, it would seem to be more important to consider the extent of colonization and the ultimate dwelling places of these peoples rather than were their forebears began. After all, it would seem reasonable to expect that Noah's family exited the Ark together, dwelt in some proximity to the Ark, were none too distant from one another, and initially did not ven-

ture too far away from Mount Ararat! By the time of Ezekiel, the dominant empire around the Mediterranean Sea was not Assyria or Babylon – it was *Phoenicia* – the secular name used for the Canaanites. Some say the Phoenician Empire even reached to the new world by the time of Solomon!

To make the point more explicit, I developed a detailed chart in the prequel to this book owing to the research by Tim Osterholm and his magnificent study that incorporating the work of almost 30 scholars (modern as well as ancient), identifying where great peoples originated and where they "wound up". His research was based (among others) upon the scholarship of John F. Walvoord, Lambert Dolphin Jr., Paul F. Taylor, Ken Ham, Ray Stedman, Henry M. Morris, John C. Whitcomb, and Arthur C. Custance. Ancient scholars consulted included Herodotus, Strabo, and Josephus (Appendix II lists ancient references demonstrating – *before* the time of Ezekiel – that scholars understood *the domain of Magog extended far beyond Anatolia*).

The other key issue related to genealogy and the names in Ezekiel concerns the issue of whether the reference to Rosh constitutes a reference to "Rus", i.e., the Russians (which means the "land of the Rus"), or whether it's strictly an adjective meaning *chief* as in "chief prince" or "chief priest". *"Behold, I am against you, O Gog, prince of **Rosh**, Meshech and Tubal."* This topic remains a subject of great debate. If *Rosh* references Russia it deals a death blow to the Islamic Antichrist Theory because the Theory in no small part depends upon the core assertion that Turkey, an Islamic Nation, must be the leader of the pack in Ezekiel 38 *and not Russia*.

In the conventional view, Russia comprises the leader and it doesn't matter whether it exists as an atheistic nation or Christian one (depending upon your confidence in the revival of the Eastern Orthodox Church as a genuine force in Russian governance and culture). While true that many former Soviet Union nations like Tajikistan and Turkmenistan remain mostly Muslim and continue to have strong ties with Moscow to this day, their influence on what happens in the Kremlin most likely lies somewhere between *slight* to *nil*. In other words, Muslims do not control Russia.

Opponents to the IAT continue to argue that Russia, not Turkey, is the instigator of the War of Gog and Magog, and that God Himself hooks Gog in the jaws, "turning him back" and "drawing him into" the conflict leading to the attack on Israel. The list of conventional scholars speaking on *behalf of Russia and against Turkey* as the leader of the confederation is most impressive, even more than the list Richardson produces: Arnold Fruchtenbaum, Rabbi Moshe Eisemann, Mark Hitchcock, Thomas Ice, Grant Jeffrey Jack Kelley, Hal Lindsey, Thomas McCall, Zola Levitt, J. Dwight Pentecost, John Mark Ruthven, John F. Walvoord, Bill Salus, J.R. Church, Gary Stearman, John Price, and yours truly.

Remember there are *two enormous and improbable geopolitical challenges that the Islamic Antichrist Theory must overcome.*

The first improbable supposition: Turkey leads Islam against Israel *while Russia and the United States "sit out" the conflict*. Geopolitically, a Turkish move implies Russia and the U.S. have no interests in the region and no intention to oppose Turkey in leading an Islamic War against Israel.

The second improbable supposition: *Turkey and Iran overcome their differences and work together, Sunni and Shia, to annihilate and disperse the Jews in Israel.* There is little ancient or modern precedent for such cooperation. Observing what has happened recently in the political executions of 43 Shia in Eastern Saudi Arabia (by the Sunni government) or Western Iraq (by the crimes of Shia against Sunni and vice versa) demonstrates that the hatred between Shia and Sunni continues unabated. It seems genuine – ISIS would never have arisen if it were concocted.

While Ezekiel 38:13 can be (and usually is) interpreted to indicate that Sheba and Dedan (Saudi Arabia), the Merchants of Tarshish (England), and its young lions (the U.S.) won't engage in the Gog and Magog war, (being puzzled as to what Gog's military action means) this particular verse says nothing about Russia sitting out the dance. That would be beyond the realm of possibility. And if Turkey were to make the move without NATO, or for NATO and the U.S. to sit by and do nothing in response to Turkey leading an Islamic attack on Israel, it also transcends any geopolitical reality the wildest imagination could conjecture. Therefore, it would seem clear that:

(1) Russia leads the confederation against Israel (Gog being the Prince of Rosh as the conventional position argues); and

(2) The United States and the United Kingdom are not in any position to react to the aggression mounted by Russia and its allies.

(3) Saudi Arabia is also directly and negatively impacted by what Russia and Iran (Persia) do when they mount an assault against Israel.

Even if the Bible were to be interpreted so that Turkey equates with Gog, geopolitically speaking (that is, based upon the realities of world politics at this time), the fundamental scenario argued by the purveyors of Islamic Antichrist Theory remains flawed to its core. (I will expound upon the geopolitical issues further in the next section.)

Again, the tribal names in Ezekiel no doubt reference the sons of Japheth and where they originally settled, many of which remained for an indefinite period of time. What remains at stake is whether Ezekiel's list of names references only their most ancient home or whether it's adumbrative (prophetic). Does the list refer to the descendants of these peoples and where they dwelt at the time Ezekiel prophesied (nearly 2,000 years afterwards)? Or does it refer to the future, over 4,500 years later in the "last days", when the prophecy is to be fulfilled?

Just for a refresher, the area we know as Anatolia did not stay static. It would be transformed into a series of distinct provinces during Greek and Roman times, with cities whose names would become familiar to Christians as the cities of the seven churches in Revelation, such as Ephesus, Philadelphia, Pergamum, Sardis, and Laodicea. As the map of the Seleucid Empire shown earlier (during the Hasmonean Dynasty), the place names across Assyria and Turkey became distinctly different.

## 8. The Muslim Mahdi, the Dajjāl, and the Antichrist are confused.

Nowadays, many students of Bible prophecy would suppose that if the Muslim *Mahdi* were to be revealed, he would be the Antichrist, expressing all manner of blasphemy against Jesus, the Son of God. However, most Christians would be surprised to learn that Muslims believe Jesus will appear in the end times and that Muslims will revere him!

Islamic prophecy mentions Jesus, within which he is known by the name *Isa*. In fact, while the Mahdi will lead the Islamic Kingdom of Allah during seven years of peace, it is Isa that kills the Muslim antichrist, Dajjāl, and then reigns almost six times longer than the Mahdi, for 40 years. The Mahdi is a prophet filled with the spirit of Mohammed, but in the last days Isa (Jesus) ranks higher than Mohammed.

In contrast, IAT appears to suggest that Islamic prophecy may appear to Muslims as if it is being fulfilled in the last days, but the true identity these personages represent *is reversed*. Curiously, Muslims may view the Dajjāl as their antichrist, but according to Chris White, Joel Richardson asserts that this Dajjāl will represent *the true Christ*. How could this be? Is White overstating what Richardson has said?

At issue is whether this one instance of mistaken identity is based on genuine support from the *Quran* and the hadiths, or whether it has been generated from Richardson's own analysis of the Islamic Antichrist. Has Richardson unintentionally facilitated the "crossover" of Christian prophecy into the Muslim domain?

It is purported in the IAT that Muslims in fact regard the "rider of the white horse" in Revelation 6 as the *Mahdi* (while Christians often assert this horseman symbolizes the Antichrist). Is this actually the case? Furthermore, has Richardson identified the Dajjāl as the inverse of the true Christ? Do Muslim and Christian prophecies hold this image in common, even if they are "inverse" in respect to one another?

In his book seeking to debunk the Islamic Antichrist Theory, author Chris White maintains that Joel Richardson proposes the Dajjāl will in fact be Christ, and misrepresents Muslim prophetic affirmation to identify the rider of the white horse in Revelation 6:1-2 as the Mahdi. This causes Chris White to make a strong allegation against Richardson and "his theory":

> I believe the Islamic Antichrist view is the most dangerous theory about the end times that has ever been proposed. I believe it surpasses all the other suspect views about the last days because it has the potential to be used so effectively by the Antichrist to convince both Jews and Christians that he is their savior. I should point out that this theory is only dangerous to those people who will live to encounter the Antichrist. It is not a dangerous belief for the average Christian; but for the people who encounter the Antichrist, it could be devastating.[29]

I am not certain that this extreme statement White makes is fair to Richardson. But to explain why he makes the statement it is best to quote White (who quotes Richardson) in a somewhat lengthy and slightly difficult passage to follow. If White is correct, however, then it's needful to track this matter down to set the record straight.

First, White cites Richardson who states the Muslim hadiths hold that the Mahdi rides on a white steed (just as many conventional Christian futurists affirm) in Revelation 6:1-2, noting the **first** *"horseman of the Apocalypse"* rides a white horse:

> Richardson says an influential Islamic scholar in the middle ages believed the Mahdi is in view in Revelation 6: 1–2 in which a rider on a white horse, typically understood to be the Antichrist, is seen. I will quote Richardson directly on this point: "For in seeing the Antichrist on the white horse with a crown and conquering, Muslim scholars see a clear picture of the Mahdi. As mentioned in the earlier chapter on the Mahdi, the early Muslim transmitter of hadiths, Ka'b al Ahbar is quoted as saying: **"I find the Mahdi recorded in the books of the Prophets... For instance, the Book of Revelation says: 'And I saw and behold a white horse. He that sat on him... went forth conquering and to conquer.'"**[30]

White goes on to point out that Richardson, while citing this quotation from one Ka'b al Ahbar, failed to distinguish between what the "early" Muslim cleric said and what two modern Egyptian authors (*Muhammad Ibn Izzat* and *Muhammad Azif*) cited him to have said in their book *Al-Mahdi* (1997). After looking up the statement and reviewing it carefully, White alleges that Richardson has *the Muslim cleric* making the comparison to Revelation 6 (the rider on the white horse), when the comparison was actually made by the two modern authors who cited al Ahbar – meaning that the hadith did not actually convey this comparison. That is, Ka'b al Ahbar did not state the latter portion of the quote (printed in **bold** above); Izzat and Azif only supposed the similarity. Subsequent Christian writers quote Richardson and carry forward the allusion that the transmitter of the hadith, al Ahbar, had said it. The ***allusion*** (an inaccurate reference) becomes an ***illusion*** (forgive the wordplay) as soon as other Christian writers assume that Richardson is in fact citing an ancient Muslim source, when he actually isn't.

Whether true or not, the point is that early Muslim hadiths *do not connect the Mahdi to the rider of the white horse in Revelation*. And the other matter would be asking Richardson to clarify his position and respond to White's allegation that Richardson was "putting words in the pen" (so to speak) of Ka'b Ahbar and in the hadith. As White summarizes: "If you look up the idea of the Mahdi riding a white horse, you will not find the idea in the hadiths or the Quran. Instead, you will find Christians citing Joel Richardson who attributes the words of a recent book to the Medieval Islamic scholar Ka'b al-Ahbar."[31] If true, then White deserves credit for checking references based upon his suspicion (and extensive research) that Muslims do not hold to this point of view. And Richardson deserves a chance to respond and offer an amended viewpoint.

White goes further, however, alleging that Richardson advises Christians to accept the Dajjāl as the true Christ when the Muslims ascribe that title to their particular "antihero" personage. Again, White chafes on this point, arguing that because the Dajjāl is a creation of false Islamic eschatology, it could be a massive mistake to draw such a conclusion. Regarding Richardson's position, White indicates Richardson provides such counsel in his book, *Mideast Beast*. No specific page number citation is given, however, so I would suspend judgment against Richardson on this point. Nevertheless, it is this last statement that causes White to express such antagonism regarding what Richardson may or may not hold to be true.

## 9. The War of Gog and Magog is not the same as Armageddon; Gog and Antichrist are not the same person.

While there is some need for caution in making too much of what Richardson communicated regarding the Dajjāl, there is little doubt that Richardson and Shoebat express clearly the view that the wars of Gog/Magog and Armageddon are the same war, and the distinct personages conventional eschatology knows as Gog and Antichrist are, from the IAT's position, the very same person. This most certainly breaks from the standard scenario.

In my book, *The Next Great War in the Middle East*, I provide two separate charts identifying the distinctive characteristics of the personages and the wars. I won't reprint them here, but I will summarize why I believe IAT is wrong to conflate the battles and the personages.

Concerning the differences of the Wars of Gog/Magog and the War of Armageddon and their respective leaders, these points seem to clearly distinguish the events:

- One, (Gog/Magog) appears to occur at the beginning or before Daniel's 70th Week, the other (Armageddon) happens at the conclusion of the 70th week;

- Gog/Magog includes selected and named nations, Armageddon includes nations from all over the globe;
- Gog leads the attack from the North, the Antichrist may attack from multiple directions (Daniel 11 does not necessarily apply as we shall see) while the "Kings of the East" enter the theater from the East;
- Gog clearly leads the Gog/Magog War (by definition) while the Antichrist leads the war against Christ in Armageddon.
- The nature of destruction appears to be distinct: Gog/Magog may be destroyed by fire and brimstone from heaven; the armies of Antichrist are destroyed by the Word of Jesus' mouth.
- The dead are buried in the Valley of Hamongog over a "seven month" period in the first war, while the dead at the conclusion of the War of Armageddon are not expressly stated to continue in the field for such a long period of time.
- Gog is buried with his armies; Antichrist is thrown into the Lake of Fire with the False Prophet.
- There is no indication that Israel incurs destruction in the Gog/Magog war while the Armageddon campaign causes Israel to lose two-thirds of its population through death or dispersion.
- The Jews are told to flee the Antichrist; they are not told to flee from Gog.
- Gog attacks Israel (potentially for spoil depending upon how one interprets Ezekiel 38:10-12); Antichrist attacks Israel to destroy Israel and decimate the Jews.
- God appears to draw Gog into the War of Gog/Magog for the glory of His name and to declare Himself the God of the Jews; the Antichrist ultimately enters the land of Israel to make war with Israel's Messiah and His people Israel.

I also point out that there is a predecessor/successor relationship between these wars. One war must happen *before the other can*. Quoting from my book, *The Next Great War in the Middle East*:

The War of Gog and Magog must become a geopolitical necessity if the Antichrist and his one-world government are to come to fruition. The greatest obstacles to this world government and its singular leader are these:

- Russia's drive to restore its empire (its nationalist agenda), which opposes globalism as currently led by the United States;
- Islam's goal of a global caliphate, along with the implicit destruction of all other religions and governments opposing Islam.
- The voice of the American people who oppose globalism, the abrogation of the U.S. constitution, and stand for individual liberty and freedom, which those seeking a one-world government would never allow.

The Battle of Gog and Magog will eliminate all three of these obstacles:

- The lands of Sheba and Dedan (Saudi Arabia), the Merchants of Tarshish (England), and its young lions (the United States) will be attacked by a great power from the north. Unless an unexpected and unforeseen transformation occurs, the U.S. and perhaps England as well awaits a destiny likened to "Sodom and Gomorrah" [according to the Prophets]
- The principal powers of Islam that team with Russia (primarily Iran, but perhaps Turkey... would all likely share Gog's fate. If they join the confederation, they will be destroyed on the mountains of Israel along with Gog's military mustered for battle.
- And then God will judge Russia (Gog) for its attack on Israel and upon the daughter of Babylon. *"And I will send a fire on Magog, and among them that dwell carelessly in the isles: and they shall know that I am the LORD."* (Ezekiel 39:6).

## 10. The Jews will never accept a Muslim as their promised Messiah.

One of the core premises of the conventional scenario is that the Antichrist presents himself to the Jewish nation, a nation regathered and rebirthed in the Holy Land, and he is accepted (or comes to be seen by many) as the promised Messiah.

Jesus said in John 5:43, *"I am come in my Father's name, and ye receive me not: if another shall come in his own name, him ye will receive."* This statement has always seemed a veiled prophecy that while the Jews rejected Christ (*"He came unto His own and his own received Him not"*, John 1:11), the Antichrist would present himself to the Jews and the Jews would accept him. But is it clear that this person would present himself literally as the Messiah, the one of whom the prophets spoke? Christians have always held that in some sense the Antichrist would make such a claim in a restored Temple in Jerusalem. Paul called him "the man of lawlessness" and the "son of perdition"; John referred to him as the "first beast" in Revelation 13, and Daniel would describe his attributes through names such as the "the willful King" and "the man of fierce countenance". Jesus' statement might have no future reference beyond that of Simon bar Kokhba and his revolt foiled by Rome in 135 A.D. From other studies, we know that the Bar Kokhba Rebellion led to the revision of the Jewish calendar by a disciple of Rabbi Akiva in an attempt to prove Simon was the long-awaited Messiah.[32] The "adjustment" accounts for most of the *missing 243 years in the Jewish calendar* (when compared to secular history).

Daniel's 70th week centers on a covenant that is confirmed at the beginning of this final week of years, the *shabuwa*. At the mid-way point (3.5 years), the Antichrist appears in the Temple and proclaims Himself God, desolating the Temple and thereby becoming the Abomination of Desolation spoken of by Daniel the Prophet. We read in Daniel 9:27,

> *And he shall confirm the covenant with many for one week: and in the midst of the week he shall cause the sacrifice and the oblation to cease, and for the overspreading of abominations he shall make it desolate, even until the consummation, and that determined shall be poured upon the desolate.*

Perhaps his presentation of himself to the Jewish people would be similar to how President Barack Obama presented himself on Palm Sunday, March 22, 2013 during ceremonies entitled the "Brit Amin" – the "unbreakable alliance" – in which Obama and Benjamin Netanyahu pledged a union that could not be broken.

Many wondered whether this ceremony was in fact the pledging of the covenant, the confirmation that would commence the final shabuwa of Daniel's prophecy. Since that time, however, no real evidence has been demonstrated that a covenant was made or confirmed which has any significance, as has been literally contemplated by eschatology scholars for many centuries. We know that President Obama was raised as a Muslim and clearly has favorable sentiments toward the Islamic faith, going out of his way to assure Muslims that the United States is not a Christian nation any longer, implying (apparently) it is not a nation that would discriminate against Islam.

But during this time, it has also been clear to Benjamin Netanyahu that Obama does not like him and does not wish to maintain the same type of relationship as other Presidents have had with Israel. While military support will be continued, pressure grows year-by-year for Israel to accept a two-state solution if it wishes to continue receiving U.S. aid. If this "unbreakable alliance", the covenant between the U.S. and Israel, were to break down, now would seem to be the perfect time. The tension between the two governments has never been greater.

Rumors circulate today (April 2016) that the U.S. will push for a vote at the Security Council of the U.N. to establish Palestine not just as a recognized state (which from the U.N.'s perspective it already is) but that the U.N. will declare the Palestinian capital to be *East Jerusalem*. If the Security Council (heavily influenced by the five permanent member states which of course include the U.S. and Russia) makes this decision, it cannot be easily undone as it binds all parties and subsequently, all parties would have to agree to reverse the decision.

Netanyahu would be furious with Obama's "farewell gift" as he leaves the U.S. Presidency. Therefore, if the Antichrist were necessarily someone viewed favorably by the Jews, Obama would hardly appear to be that man of the hour – certainly not in the mind of the current Israeli Administration. Obama does not appear to be the one who would make or confirm a covenant with the Jews, promising peace, and bestowing the right to go forward with the building of a new Jewish temple on the Temple Mount. If Obama should go on, after his presidency, to become Secretary General of the U.N. which some speculate he intends, all bets are off and all decisions subject to revision.

Meanwhile we are reading more and more that Turkey's President Recep Tayyip Erdoğan wishes to re-establish diplomatic ties with Israel and normalize relations. On March 22, 2016, in the aftermath of the terrorist attack in Belgium, Erdoğan spoke of his willingness to work closely with Israel to address the evilness of terrorism. Citing statements from the *Jerusalem Post*, March 23, 2016,

> "I believe that against this terrorism we have to stand together with the international community and take a very very firm stance and increase our cooperation against all terrorist acts," Erdoğan told Israel President Reuven Rivlin.
>
> For his part, Rivlin thanked Erdoğan for his condolences, and expressed his sorrow to Turkey in light of the [recent] suicide bombing that killed four people. "Terror is terror, life is life, and blood is blood, whether it is in Istanbul, Brussels, Paris or Jerusalem," Rivlin said. "We must all stand together in the fight against this terrible evil."

Islamic Antichrist Theorists also assert some form of agreement *must be confirmed by the Antichrist,* and Shoebat continues to declare Erdoğan the Antichrist: (1) whether or not he has or will present himself as the Mahdi; (2) has or will be designated as Messiah based upon his actions or claims; or (3) merely commits to protect Israel in some manner from military threats of other nations in the region.

The extent of the agreement remains unclear but must be significant enough to fulfill the covenant of Daniel 9 that will be broken in the "middle of the week".

Many have volunteered the axiom that the Jews would never accept a Muslim as their Messiah. It is hard to argue with that logic; however, it is not necessarily obvious from scripture that the Antichrist will claim he is a Jew. That issue deserves a separate study. And yet, it is conceivable that the Israeli government could make a deal with a leader who has a Muslim background (like Obama)[33] or is currently the leader of a Muslim country (like Erdoğan) and *confirm a covenant*, which is broken in the middle of the 70th week, and through which this world leader becomes the desolater, the "reincarnation" of the Seleucid Antiochus Ephiphanes IV, who committed the Abomination of Desolation in 165 B.C., during the Maccabean Revolt. This new Antiochus could launch a new war against the Jews to fulfill this prophecy once again.

But is this new Antiochus, *the King of the North* as spoken of in Daniel 11? Or is he the "third king" aka the "willful king?" Who is this King of the North and is he a genuine part of prophetic type of the Antichrist of the last days? Or is this aspect of the conventional scenario *an error in prophetic interpretation* that has been carried forward for decades without question?

Historically the identity of this King of the North has been associated with Assyria, and more specifically with both Nimrod, and his descendent Sennacharib. But Islamic Antichrist Theory concludes that since Assyria once controlled a good portion of Turkey in the eighth century B.C., the *leader of Turkey will turn out to be this future King of the North* as designated by Daniel (and presumed to be prophesied in Daniel 11 and fulfilled at the time of the end). Additionally, Islamic Antichrist Theory believes the King of the North is NOT distinct from "the King" discussed later in Daniel 11 (verses 36-45), a king who appears to assume attributes expressly reserved *for the Antichrist*. Thus, for Islamic Antichrist Theorists, *the Antichrist and the King of the North are one and the same*. For most conventional theorists, the Antichrist is not the King of the North, but "the willful King" beginning in verse 36.

So the IAT does not represent the conventional understanding of Daniel 11 as IAT assumes there are but "two kings" (or kingly lines) rather than "three kings" as proffered by the standard interpretation of Daniel 11. Whether Daniel 11:36-45 will be realized in space-time events as depicted there (or as we will discuss, WAS fulfilled two millennia ago), it points out another distinction between Islamic Antichrist Theory and conventional futurist thinking.

Commentator Jack Kelly provides a concise and insightful review of the primary passages of Daniel 11, disclosing the identities of *the three kings of convention* and why the King of the North is not identified as the Antichrist. His is the "conventional" Futurist view. First we recite with him, the two essential verses of Daniel 11:

- *"The king will do as he pleases. He will exalt and magnify himself above every god and will say unheard-of things against the God of gods. He will be successful until the time of wrath is completed, for what has been determined must take place" ( verse 36).*

- *"At the time of the end the king of the South will engage him in battle, and the king of the North will storm out against him with chariots and cavalry and a great fleet of ships. He will invade many countries and sweep through them like a flood" (verse 40.)*

Three separate kings are in view in **Daniel 11:36** & **40** and their identities must be discovered to fully understand what will happen in the days leading up to the End of the Age. They are the [1] King who exalts himself, the [2] King of the North, and the [3] King of the South. All of **Daniel 11:4-35** has been taken up with a discussion of various generations of the King of the North and the King of the South. *The King who exalts himself is neither, and yet subdues them both.* Let's see if we can identify these three kings as to their roles in the world's final drama.

First, the King who exalts himself. The angel told Daniel this king would exalt and magnify himself above every god (Daniel 11:36). In 2 Thessalonians 2:4 Paul said the anti-Christ [would] exalt himself over everything that is called god or is worshiped. The angel also told Daniel he would say unheard of things against the God of gods. In Rev. 13:6 John said the anti-Christ [would] blaspheme God and slander His name. *So it looks like the king who exalts himself is the anti-Christ.* [Emphasis mine] 34

Preterist scholarship, however, rules out the possibility that the prophecies of Daniel 11 pertain to a *future* Antichrist. It presents a strong case that all of the prophecies were fulfilled in the three centuries leading up to the First Advent of Christ. Since it considers the fulfillment historical (and NOT future), *it agrees with neither convention nor Islamic Antichrist Theory*. Allow me to explain this third viewpoint.

All three positions agree that the first part of Daniel chapter 11 was fulfilled *before* Christ was born. It relates to the Kings of Persia and Greece including Arius, Xerxes, Alexander the Great, and Alexander's kingdom that, after his untimely death, was divided into four parts in order for each of his generals to obtain a share (those generals being Cassander, Lysimachus, Seleucus, and Ptolemy). The only disagreement among scholars is whether this section of Daniel was prophetic (truly recorded by Daniel in the fifth century B.C.), or was in fact written after the fact, by the Maccabees some time after 165 B.C. to portray themselves as the heroic warriors battling Antiochus IV Epiphanes. Liberal scholarship asserts this latter view, a *non-orthodox* position based on mistrusting any supernatural element in Bible prophecy (the ability to foretell the future). 35

All three positions, presume that the King of the North changes to Seleucus and his successors – whose empire included Anatolia, Judea, and most of the Middle East even unto India. *Ptolemy* and his scions became the *King of the South*. This identification works well until we come to verse 36 and venture beyond it. Certainly the details provided in the prophecy from Daniel 11:21-35 specifically refer to Antiochus IV Ephiphanes. Once we move past verse 35 however, the matter gets much more controversial. Is the remainder of the chapter future or does it still prophesy events happening before Jesus' birth?

In reviewing the issue of "the three kings" of Daniel 11:36-45, as mentioned above, I studied several resources arguing this section also has been fulfilled. They assert a future antichrist and suggest the verses here yield insight into the nature of the "final antichrist", but they provide a strong historical case that this section of Daniel was fulfilled completely *by King Herod just before Jesus was born*. One such scholar is the famed Preterist Philip Mauro (1859-1952), but a more recent author is the late Bryan Huie (d. 2012). Mauro and Huie exposit Daniel 11:21-35 similarly, demonstrating that Antiochus IV Epiphanes fulfilled those verses in detail. *"And in his place shall arise a vile person, to whom they will not give the honor of royalty; but he shall come in peaceably, and seize the kingdom by intrigue"* (Daniel 11:21, NKJV). But beginning with 11:36, the story moves on to the actions of Herod, the King of the Jews at the time of the birth of Jesus who (feeling threatened) infamously murdered untold numbers of infants (two years and under) in Judea to protect his throne from conquest by the Son of David, the Messiah whom the "Three Wise Men" from the east (probably Babylon) sought. At this point and then throughout the rest of Daniel 11, the *King of the North* becomes *Octavian* (we know him best as Caesar Augustus), operating from Seleucia (composed mostly of ancient Assyria) but *acting on behalf of Rome*. The King of the South is no longer Ptolemy and his scions, but Mark Antony in confederation with his true love, the infamous Cleopatra of Egypt.

To reiterate, the history recited by Mauro and Huie presents a strong case that all the material in Daniel 11 covers history up *to the first Advent of Christ but not beyond*. Here is Huie's perspective regarding how well King Herod fits the description of "the King" (a third but sole monarch):

> *"And the king shall do as he wills. He shall exalt himself and magnify himself above every god, and shall speak astonishing things against the God of gods. He shall prosper till the indignation is accomplished*; for what is decreed shall be done" (Daniel 11:36, ESV).
>
> In this verse, the king being spoken of changes. Starting in verse 21, Antiochus IV Epiphanes was the referenced king. Verses 32 through 35 prophesy his defeat by the Maccabees (the Hasmoneans) and encompass the subsequent fall of their dynasty. But the context shows that the remaining verses in this chapter cannot apply to Antiochus IV.
>
> Most Christian scholars try to insert a huge chronological gap in the prophecy here, making the rest of it apply not to the antetype Antiochus IV, but to the end-time type, the Antichrist. But staying in the time sequence context earlier alluded to by Gabriel (Dan. 11:1), what should we expect to see next in this prophecy? Was there a king who ruled Israel after the end of the Hasmonean era?
>
> What appears to have caused scholars to stray away from the correct understanding at this point of the prophecy is that they were unable to find a successor to Antiochus IV who matched the description of "the king." But two points must be kept in mind in order to properly understand this prophecy. The subject is the Seleucid or Ptolemaic dynasties ONLY as these kingdoms affected Daniel's people. Therefore, the expression "the king," without any other description, could certainly mean one who was king over Israel. Secondly, the immediately preceding verses (Dan. 11:32-35) refer to the Jews and their situation during and after the Maccabean revolt. Based on the history of this period, we should look for the fulfillment of this verse by a "king" other than Antiochus IV or the Hasmonean rulers.
>
> Both secular history and the New Testament record the acts of a king who appeared on the scene in Israel at the end of the Hasmonean period. As we shall see, this king fulfilled every prophetic description given in verses 36 through 39. **That king was Herod the Great.** In verse 36, the one spoken of is not identified as either the king of the North or the king of the South, but simply as "the king." Herod was seated as king on the throne of Israel when Messiah Yeshua was born. He is the called "the king" in the Gospels (Matt. 2:1, 3, 9; Luke 1:5). He, like Antiochus IV before him, was an antetype of the coming Antichrist, as his actions revealed. [36] [Emphasis added]

Huie goes on to chronicle the historical details of Herod's reign of terror [37] continuing beyond verse 39, completing the details of Herod's fulfillment of the Daniel 11 prophecies for the remainder of the chapter through verse 45. Two examples provided by Huie provide insight into how King Herod fulfilled two of the more memorable prophecies in Daniel 11:

*"But in their place he shall honor a god of fortresses; and a god which his fathers did not know he shall honor with gold and silver, with precious stones and pleasant things."* (Daniel 11:38, NKJV)

Herod's actions in securing and holding on to power provide an impressive fulfillment of this verse. The phrase "god of forces," or "fortresses," is uncommon enough that it provides us a ready means of identification. The Roman emperors proclaimed themselves to be "gods," and it was by their military "forces" or "fortresses" that they enlarged and sustained their power and their empire. Herod was quick to honor the warring Roman rulers with tribute and building projects. He rebuilt many fortresses in the land and temples in surrounding Gentile areas, including three temples dedicated to Caesar Augustus. He rebuilt the ancient Phoenician coastal fort called Strato's Tower and renamed it Caesarea in honor of Caesar Augustus;[38] he rebuilt Samaria, and renamed it Sebaste (**sebastos** was the Greek word for "reverend," equivalent to the Latin **augustus**). He built many other fortified cities and named them in honor of Caesar...

*"Thus he shall act against the strongest fortresses with a foreign god, which he shall acknowledge, and advance its glory; and he shall cause them to rule over many, and divide the land for gain."* (Daniel 11:39)

Verse 39 continues the subject from the previous verse. Using the support and backing of the Roman emperor, Herod was able to overcome all of his foes. In the process, he promoted the glory of the Romans in Judea to his own benefit. Herod gave land and authority to those who supported him in order to secure their allegiance. When viewed properly, we can see that every item foretold of "the king" in verses 36-39 was fulfilled in the reign of Herod.

I encourage readers to study Bryan Huie's works at www.*herealittletherealittle.net* and compare to Philip Mauro's exposition in *The Seventy Weeks and the Great Tribulation*.

Scholars who take this "Preterist" position on all of Daniel 11 (that is, that it has all been fulfilled), still assert there will be an Antichrist in the last days, and thus they continue to see Daniel 9:24-27 speaking of future prophecies about Antichrist and Messiah, some of which are yet to be fulfilled (specifically, sealing up of vision and prophecy as well as the anointing of the Messiah). However, they eliminate Daniel 11 from future detail fulfillment in "space-time" and assert it's mistaken to include these prophecies (except for the unholy attributes of Antiochus and "the King" applying to the future Antichrist). Therefore, if this view is correct, the debate about whether there are two kings or three in Daniel 11:36-45 when predicting the movements of the last days' Antichrist (i.e., the movements of the King of the North and the King of the South as well as "hearing rumors and pitching tents") becomes moot. Instead, Daniel 11 relates *entirely* to the history of the Jewish people leading up to the *first coming of their Messiah*.

If we accept this third position concerning Daniel 11 as depicted by Mauro and Huie (and I am strongly inclined to do so), many confusing aspects of futurist eschatology are resolved. As it relates to the Islamic Antichrist Theory, simply put, the notion that the Islamic Mahdi becomes the final King of the North in Daniel 11 is entirely shunted. All of the characters and all of the actions described in minute detail by Daniel are "taken off the table" as they have been fulfilled 2,000 years ago as he prophesied.

Note: IAT employs the "two king" theory of Daniel 11 to reinforce their position that in the last days, there are two Muslim groups – not the Shia and the Sunni – but *a northern alliance led by Turkey and a southern alliance led by Egypt*. Richardson argues that Turkey (aligned with Iran) will move against Egypt (aligned with the Saudis, the Sudan and Libya). Articulated years ago, his position has been complicated by the geopolitical developments of the Arab Spring, and the fact that most recently, Egypt has taken a back seat and Saudi Arabia teaming with Turkey to stare down Syria and Russia. My main point here: If we acknowledge that all of Daniel 11 is historical, and only the *attributes* of "the king" are "double fulfilled" applying to the future Antichrist, IAT loses a vital plank from its platform.[39] The "King of the North" is no longer an item!

What then should be our view of Daniel 11? Do we harm the value of Bible prophecy by challenging the issue of whether or not Daniel 11:36-45 remains future? Not at all. The sheer number of historically verified prophecies in the Book of Daniel and its chapter 11 stands as a vital and impressive proof of the Bible's truth, which we should relish. It adds strong support to the prophecies of Daniel 9 (and elsewhere) that still await future fulfillment.

Even if we stipulate that the Islamic Antichrist is both the Islamic Mahdi as well as Gog of Ezekiel 38-39 (which I am not willing to do), the confusion surrounding the King of the North (which confounds all futurist scholars from my vantage point) dissipates quickly. *Only certain aspects* of these antitypes of the Antichrist, Antiochus IV Epiphanes (the Greek Seleucid) and King Herod (the Idumean) both of who have strong ties to Rome, *find their ultimate fulfillment in the personage of the Antichrist yet future.* The manner of his attacks and the sequence of movements in "the Beautiful Land" (Judea) supplied by the prophecies of Daniel 11, which most futurists struggle to associate with either Gog or the future Beast, *do not apply to the future son of perdition at all,* since Antiochus IV and Herod the Great have fulfilled them. Therefore, historical details in Daniel 11 don't apply to Antichrist – only the *attributes* of these evil antitypes.

In concluding this section, we should note that the two antitypes of the Antichrist in Daniel 11, Antiochus IV and Herod, *were not Jews.* They were in fact hated rulers of the Jews. Herod would hail the God of the Jews as "our Father" but he stated this for political reasons and perhaps even to mock the Jews. If the Antichrist has Jewish lineage (which he likely does as J.R. Church argues in his *book Daniel Reveals the Bloodline of the Antichrist*), these antitypes would suggest that the "Jewishness" of Antichrist is not part of his appeal to Israel. It could possibly remain hidden. It may never be a part of a *covenant confirmation* marking the beginning of Daniel's 70th week. *It might not ever be disclosed.*

One last point: Islamic Antichrist Theorists insist that Daniel's four kingdoms (in Daniel 7) do not include Rome but instead refer to the Ottoman Empire as the fourth and final empire. Of course I disagree. But it should not be missed that the two antitypes we have just considered, Antiochus and Herod, *both ruled under the aegis of Rome.* Therefore, once again, to suppose that Rome does not merit mention as the fourth beast (aka empire) of Daniel 7 remains yet one more puzzling and contradictory aspect of the Islamic Antichrist view. That the Ottoman Empire comprises the fourth beast is ruled out entirely, since by definition, there can only be one "fourth beast"!

# Part Three:
# Geopolitical Realities Challenging the Islamic Antichrist Theory

## Why Geopolitics Mandates Russia and Not Turkey Will Be Gog of Magog

READERS OF MY BLOGS AND BOOKS KNOW THAT I EXPRESS WORRY THAT RUSSIA HAS BEEN BACKED INTO A CORNER ECONOMICALLY AND WILL COME OUT SWINGING. PROPHETICALLY, I argue that this is one of the key geopolitical reasons I finger Russia as the leader of the Muslim nations in the Ezekiel war known as the War of Gog and Magog. There are many scriptural reasons for taking this position, some straightforward while some require scholastic study and a dose of spiritual insight. Author Joel Richardson has done a masterful job building a strong scriptural base for his viewpoint in his books, *The Islamic Antichrist* and *Mideast Beast*. However, the appeal of the Islamic Antichrist Theory grows considerably weaker when one studies the realities of modern history, geopolitics, and the geographical rock-hard factoids we know as mountains, oceans, rivers, and the vast steppes of Europe and Asia.

We usually reckon that *geopolitics* (the political science of the entire globe) can either challenge or reinforce our theories regarding scriptural truths. In the case of who the likely players are in the War of Gog and Magog, geography and geopolitics have much to say concerning the most probable participants. Simply put, enormous factors outside scriptural exegesis argue *against* the Islamic Antichrist Theory (IAT). IAT runs headlong into irresistible geopolitical realities and immovable geographical objects. They are not easy to sidestep.

When we examine the history of Russia, its geography, and the current geopolitical situation in the world today, we see why Russia comprises the mostly likely leader of the nations listed in Ezekiel 38-39.

First off, it's extremely difficult to mount a credible argument that a Sunni-dominated Turkey would find itself capable of leading Shi'ite dominated nations, while at the same time staving off challenges from ambitious and determined Russian forces in the Middle East. Despite Turkey possessing the tenth strongest ranked military, its weaponry remains conventional and the Turkish navy is a non-factor. If attacked, Turkey has access to NATO's nuclear weapons, but it does not have autonomous control of these munitions. On the other hand, Russia possesses the number two-ranked military globally, has approximately three times as many tanks and pieces of artillery, a larger ground force, and of course, has the world's largest nuclear arsenal both in strategic and tactical nuclear weapons. Russia has its full nuclear arsenal at its disposal at any time. And Russia's nuclear weapons appear to be more sophisticated than those of the U.S. as I have demonstrated elsewhere and has been confirmed by experts in the field like the Washington Beacon's Bill Gertz and friend (former WND journalist and author J.R. Nyquist). Plus, Mr. Putin doesn't need the approval of anyone outside of the Kremlin to go to war and to use these massively destructive munitions as he sees fit.

Of course, Turkey remains strategically important to the United States and is a "first world" nation, which offers a large land buffer against Russian incursion into the Balkans (Southern Europe), supports efforts to keep Western Ukraine from being dominated by Moscow, and provides a maritime "chokepoint" via the Bosporus at Istanbul (where Europe meets Asia),

Turkey always presents a threat to Russia's Navy at Sevastopol in Crimea since Turkey could block the Bosporus and keep the Russian Navy locked out of the Mediterranean, meaning it could be restricted and rendered incapable of deployment beyond the Black Sea. Turkey constitutes a more stable state than any other Muslim nation in the region. It has been "Westernized" to a great extent since the end of the Ottoman Empire in 1924, transforming itself into a governmental system similar to Western states. It has been an important NATO ally for many years occupying what was once known as Asia Minor.

However, there are limits to Turkish power; and Turkey, under Recep Tayyip Erdoğan, has moved culturally "backward" (from a Western point of view) to reinstate cultural and behavioral mores of Islam. Also, Turkey frequently does not act in accordance to Washington's demands, as we will cite here.

Russia remains dangerous for a variety of reasons, most of them due to economic pressures. Historically, a key issue has been that Russia's peoples and economy are based in its most western region extending along a line from St. Petersburg to the Caucasus Mountains (which lie between the Black and Caspian Seas) in the south. This most populous and industrialized area has proven vulnerable to attack through the centuries due to vast plains that exist in Eastern Europe and in Western Russia (aka *the steppes*), meaning that there are no natural barriers like vast rivers, seas, or mountain ranges. We have seen this play out especially over the past 200 years, from the Napoleon's disastrous invasion of Russian at the beginning of the

**The Austro –Hungarian Empire (Circa 1900)**

nineteenth century; into the twentieth century through World War I when Germany and the Austro-Hungarian Empires joined forces against it; and in particular with the massive (and equally disastrous) Nazi invasion during War World II.

The Cold War can be understood in no small part by recognizing that Russia seeks to establish and retain a vast land buffer to protect the Motherland against future European invasions and covert Western incursions in its affairs. Today's squabbles over Ukraine are due to much the same Russian concern. To elaborate: the Ukraine has always been vital to Russia for several reasons: it is the "breadbasket of Europe" with some of the best agricultural soil in the world; it provides a land buffer in a post-Cold War world; it now possesses the vast oil and gas pipelines that supply Russian oil to Europe (responsible for over half of Russian government revenues); and lastly, eastern Ukraine plus Crimea provide Russia access to the Black Sea – and through it – the Mediterranean. Russia's northern most port of Murmansk is useful only part of the year (when its waters aren't frozen over); while its port at St. Petersburg is easily "choked off" through the narrow corridor passing through the Baltic Sea, and then beyond running through the waters near the Baltic States and Denmark.

An article by the respected political scientist George Friedman written for *Mauldin Economics*, published on January 25, 2016, provided a geographical explanation for what makes Russians who they are – i.e., "Spartans" instead of "Athenians". His article is entitled, *"Mapping Russia's Strategy."* It provides vital information along with some brilliant maps explaining why Russia is so determined to maintain Crimea – and why any threat to Crimea is a threat to all of Russia. Friedman points out why Russians are so loyal to the Motherland, recognizing as they do, their maritime vulnerabilities. He also explains their seeming mentality of "fighting to the last man" to defend their country.

The two maps here are from Friedman's article and are but two of many helpful charts found in his article.

Looking at the map of the "Cold War" Europe on the succeeding page, we can readily see the notion of a geographical buffer zone created by the Warsaw Pact states, and now how limited that zone is with all of those states no longer tied to the Soviet Union. Friedman underscores that Russia is especially dangerous because of how its geography creates a virtual land-locked status (if threatened, it will react in a massive way).

## The Situation in Syria

We can understand Russia's adventurous attitude in the Middle East to some extent by these geographical factors. It possesses a naval base in Syria at Tartous. It now has deployed a number of submarines off the coast of Syria which are equipped with

**Russia's Maritime Choke Points**
© Geopolitical Futures

modern cruise missiles. President Vladimir Putin has boasted that such missiles are nuclear-warhead capable. While Russia's access to the Mediterranean is limited to the Bosporus gateway at Istanbul, many Russian vessels have passed through this narrow straight and are now situated off the coast of Syria. It would be naïve to suppose the naval base in Syria is secondary to Russian interests. Russia demands this base to assure it has a substantial maritime presence without which any aspiring global power lacks ability to project power.

For all intents and purposes, these waterways are existential matters for the Russian government. Putin is in Syria for strategic reasons. He has no plans to pull his contingent out – despite the announcement in March 2016 that he is pulling back his military assets away from Syria. Au contraire! Putin also will not tolerate anyone, especially Turkey, threatening his continued presence in Syria. He will keep heavy equipment and resources at his naval and air force bases.

We cannot look at the Middle East today without sensing some very hard realities. In evaluating how the Ezekiel war would come to pass if it were to be triggered within the next two years (picking that timeframe is not entirely arbitrarily), it is very hard to see how the following geopolitical realities could be ignored. For the Islamic Antichrist Theory to be correct, it must address how these geopolitical facts can be overcome.

### 1. Russia is smack dab in the middle of the fray.

It has chosen to defend its position in Syria where it has an airbase at Latakia and more importantly, the Tartous seaport. It has placed a sizable force of planes, ships, and ground personnel to attack any and all rebels opposed to Bashar al' Assad. It has aggressively bombed targets without coordinating its efforts with the U.S. or other coalition forces. Russia will do as it pleases in Syria. Giving ground back is unrealistic.

### 2. Shi'ites are dominating the northern Middle East.

Iran is testing mid-range and long-range ballistic missiles. Iran threatens Israel but also Eastern Europe and Turkey. The probability exists that Iran already has several nuclear warheads, as does Saudi Arabia, if reports that surfaced in the March 2016 have merit. Iran appears to be breaking the rules of the "treaty" signed last July 14, 2015 with the U.S. and five other nations. Many

**The Buffer Zone of the Cold War – Present No longer**
© Geopolitical Futures

are therefore calling for sanctions to be reinstated immediately. As its critics alleged, the treaty appears to have been a grand waste of time for everyone except Iran.

## 3. The United States is operating in a "back-peddling" mode.

The U.S. government is "on its heels" as they say in basketball. The U.S. appears reactive to what is happening. Yes, it leads a coalition composed of NATO air power, but it has been applied only to very selective bombing sorties against specific Syrian rebel targets. The U.S. never directly assaulted Assad; it has fought a proxy war.

In recent months, however, the U.S. political position has been demonstrated to be duplicitous. The current administration supplied weapons to Jabhat al' Nusra, the Al Qaeda affiliate in Syria. Undoubtedly, weapons supplied by the U.S. have fallen into the hands of ISIS, supposedly our primary enemy. Many questioned just how accidental this was. Investigative reporter Seymour Hersh reported in his piece in the *London Review of Books* in January 2016, that the White House supported gun running via the CIA making use of Gaddafi's weapons cache after he was overthrown. The Pentagon opposed this action and leaked information to Germany, Israel, and Russia that it deemed would be helpful to Assad to defeat the rebels that the CIA was supporting as directed by the White House. In effect, the Pentagon was fighting against the CIA in the sands of Syria! (See Appendix 1 for more detail on this story.)

## 4. Turkey has been more foe than friend and feuds with Russia.

Turkey currently attacks the Kurds with airpower and artillery every chance it gets, despite the fact the Kurds have demonstrated themselves to be the West's best opposition to ISIS and other dangerous rebel groups. President Erdoğan has been accused of supporting ISIS by allowing truckloads of oil to pass across Turkish borders daily, enriching ISIS with millions in revenues monthly. Corruption seems to be at the heart of Turkish intent. Putin alleged this to be so and the photographic evidence of Erdoğan's deceit is accepted as true by other members of NATO and tuned-in political groups inside the U.S. Russia and Turkey have a long history of war. Tensions between the two nations continue to pop up in the news monthly.

## 5. Sunnis and Shias are on the verge of war with one another.

Sunni nations Turkey and Saudi Arabia reportedly amassed hundreds of thousands of troops along the Syrian borders in March 2016, in what appeared to be an imminent ground invasion. Operation Northern Thunder was concluded however without the predicted ground war. The threat of action appears to have had the desired effect as Russia pulled some forces out of Syria, perhaps as a reaction to this joint exercise, deescalating tensions. However, if Bashar al' Assad's regime appears likely to continue indefinitely, it's not unthinkable that Turkish and Saudi forces will again apply military pressure in the form of ground forces entering Syria. However, should another build-up occur, steps must be carefully selected, since all sides threaten use of nuclear weapons.

## 6. The U.S. has rescinded its plan to force regime change in Damascus.

The White House appears to have worked out an agreement with Russia to facilitate a future regime change. Assad has not only alienated the United States, recently Assad apparently has antagonized the Russians too, so much so that they are no longer willing to tolerate him indefinitely. Nevertheless, Vladimir Putin has once again played his hand to great effect, demonstrating new weapon systems in Syria for political benefit internally and externally, has stabilized Assad's position safeguarding Russia's strategic presence in Syria, and according to some geopolitical experts, has won compromises from the U.S. and Europe in respect to Russian interests in Crimea and Ukraine.

## 7. Israel temporarily enjoys not being at the center of hostilities.

Israel knows that this hiatus in the ongoing conflict with its neighbors is momentary; it will inevitably end once the outcome in the Syrian situation resolves to the various players' satisfaction. So why will Israel then be at greater risk? Hezbollah has taken authority over Lebanon – Hezbollah is a proxy for Iran. Syria will likely be reinforced with a new Alawite or Shia-friendly government post-Assad. Russia will bolster its presence in Syria, which is a favorable outcome for the Shia. A Shia majority in Baghdad already dominates Iraq. If the Iraqi government can find a way to mend its relationship with the Sunnis in the western Anbar province (which led to Sunni support of ISIS during the past two years), Iraq could stabilize its own internal political situation and economy in order to begin looking beyond its issues to regional matters like its perennial hatred of the Jews. Therefore, the Shi'ites have a lock across the region north of Israel. **When all of these elements have solidified (and they aren't far from doing so now), Israel will be under the gun – literally – once again.**

## 8. Russia likely to use Syria to build a stronger presence in the region.

With the most vicious of rebel groups defeated and Assad's government preserved for the time being, Russia will still be lurking to return in full force in Syria. Most Syrians (those who haven't fled to Turkey and beyond to Europe) have much in common with Westerners. They are not radical jihadis. They pursue personal wealth, well-being for their families, and a predictable lifestyle. While Russia has chosen to withdraw some of its troops and fixed-wing aircraft, it has stated it can reinstate its contingent in Syria quickly should conditions so require. As of April 2, 2016, despite the promises of withdrawal, Russia appears to be increasing its heavy equipment in Syria, as its ships are now more numerous in the Mediterranean than before the announced pull out of its military. We read the following from *Arutz Sheva* (IsraelNationalNews.com):

> Putin has continued his campaign to prop up Bashar al-Assad's regime even after the withdrawal announcement on March 14, and apparently he is intent on maintaining enough firepower on the ground to be able to rapidly escalate Russian actions if Assad is threatened.
>
> *Reuters* notes that the naval icebreaker Yauza, a main supply vessel for Russian forces in Syria, did not return to its Arctic Ocean port after Putin's announced withdrawal, but instead three days after the declaration left the Russian Black Sea for Tartous, Russia's naval facility in Syria.
>
> Photographs of the ship analyzed by the news agency showed it was carrying very heavy cargo, as it sat so low in the water its load line could barely be seen. It is unclear what exact equipment was on board.
>
> Aside from the Yauza, Russia also sent the Caesar Kunikov and the Saratov to the Mediterranean Sea shortly after the with-

drawal - both are landing ships, generally used to transport troops and armor, and both were clearly very heavily loaded.

Russia pulled around half of its fixed-wing strike force from Syria in the days after the withdrawal was announced, according to *Reuters*, but an examination of shipping data, official information, info from naval sources and photographs by bloggers of Russian ships passing the Bosphorus strait show the military buildup in Syria is not being brought to a close.

Rather it seems Russia has more war ships in the Mediterranean near the Syrian coast than at the time of Putin's announcement, with more than 12 naval craft accounted for in the region. They are there to guard cargo ships, but they likewise can fire devastating cruise missiles from the sea.[40]

There appears to be a concerted effort by Russia to accomplish significant forward placement of military equipment. Look for Russia to quietly continue to place more support vehicles and mobile artillery in the area while it maintains naval vessels and aircraft at its military installations (without much push back from the U.S.!) The trick for Russia will be to placate the Sunnis sufficiently to "keep the peace" in the region, which means finding ways to appease Turkey and Saudi Arabia, so they don't start a war that could kick off World War III.

Russia has a long history of being on the side of the Muslims against Israel. So while Israel and Russia seem now to be at a high water mark in their relationship, if conventional theory regarding Bible prophecy is true (and I am convinced it is), Russia will not maintain its detente with Israel indefinitely. Once the Shia focus outward and threaten military action against the Jews, Russia must choose with whom they will align. Smart money says it will be with the Shiites, not Israelis.

## 9. Turkey could attempt to block Russia's moves, but won't.

Turkey wishes to pursue its goal of becoming the revived Ottoman Empire. ISIS will likely become a diminished force in the area and Turkey will assert itself as the true caliphate that according to Islamic Law, all Muslims must follow. However, despite declaring itself a caliphate, which is probable at some point within the next two to four years, it seems most unlikely that Turkey would attempt any assault on Russian forces in Syria. Turkey cannot intimidate Russia. Turkey has leverage over Russia; however, it is smart enough not to exploit this leverage (as stated earlier, it could block Russian ships coming through the Bosphorus, cutting off the Russian naval base in Sevastopol). Doing so would be an act of war and Russia would absolutely do anything and everything it is power to keep its maritime point of access available. While neither Russia nor Turkey could invade the other (neither have sufficient conventional forces or the economic means to sustain such an invasion), either could launch limited assaults on strategic targets. But other than the occasional downing of a plane or sinking of a ship, we aren't likely to see major incidents.

Russia holds the trump card with tactical and strategic nuclear weapons at its disposal, alongside advanced anti-missile and anti-aircraft capability with its S-400 (remaining in place in Syria) and S-300 in Iran. Russia will soon deploy its more advanced S-500 system that offers a nuclear offensive capability as well as anti-ballistic missile defensive capability. Once this happens, nuclear weapons capability shifts the balance of power decidedly toward Moscow and away from NATO and Washington.

## 10. Oil continues to be the elephant in the room.

Controlling the oil fields and the pipelines in the Ukraine and in Syria are the matters that matter most. Virtually every economy in the world is hurting because of the low price of oil. The Saudis may have shot themselves in the foot by forcing the price of oil down. An alleged conspiracy between the House of Saud and the United States to drop the price of oil to hurt Iran and Russia appears to have backfired.

Whether there was a conspiracy between the U.S. and Saudi Arabia may never be known. But what is certain is that the current situation cannot be maintained for very long. For while the poor and the middle class enjoy the low price of oil, the economies of Saudi Arabia, Iraq, Iran, and Russia are all dramatically impacted in a negative way. If for no other reason, war looms inevitably on the horizon to force the price of oil upward and rescue the economies of these exporter nations. The issue isn't if but when. It seems the questions to be answered are who will go to war, for what reason, for what duration, and with what result. However it happens, the status quo will soon be disrupted.

## Conclusion

In Rocky III, when the fighter played by the actor (I use that term loosely) "Mr. T" was asked what he predicted for the bout between Rocky and himself, he said, "Pain!" If asked what I predict for the unstable situation in the Middle East, in a word I would forecast "War".

In the final analysis, while the poor and the middle class benefit from low gasoline prices, this matters not to the world's elite. Most informed persons understand that the well to do encourage wars to enrich themselves further. There is no reason to suspect the situation today is any different.

The Network of Russian Gas Pipelines in the Ukraine

# Appendix I:
# The Arab Spring – Five Years Later

## Overview

IT HAS BEEN FIVE YEARS SINCE A TUNISIAN STREET MERCHANT IGNITED HIS CLOTHING BURNING HIMSELF TO DEATH, AND SIMULTANEOUSLY IGNITING A FIRE THAT SOON SPREAD TO the entire Middle East. The past five years have been a watershed period for politics in the region. The developing story strongly suggests that a dramatic shift in power has occurred and will transform the region. No longer will American interests dominate the Middle East (British and French interests waned long ago). Instead, Russia will oversee the strengthening of Iran and Iraq, but more specifically Shi'ite over Sunni. Moderate Arab states are in decline. The caliphate of ISIS, despite being under heavy attack, will likely persist in some way, shape, or form to foment mischief of the most heinous kind.

We have seen an enormous alteration in U.S. political policy in the Middle East. The standard refrain used to be conflict followed by nation building, which encouraged liberty and democracy. Instead, most critics charge that America employs a strategy of ousting autocratic leaders (our former allies) and setting fire, metaphorically speaking, to the offending country's institutional structures. This picture of the United States is not one that Americans are used to seeing. Combined with the moral decay in American society that believers in Bible prophecy decry, failed U.S. foreign policy relying on often-underhanded covert operations by the CIA provokes increased alarm and a conviction to many Christians that God's judgment cannot be too far distant.

## Highlights of the Arab Spring

Let's first recap highlights of five years of "Arab Spring" and assess how this series of unfortunate events have progressed the prophetic timeline toward fulfillment.

It was December 17, 2010 when Zine el Abidine Ben Ali performed his act of immolation. Within a few weeks of that graphic incident, protests began in Egypt's Tahrir Square that led to the fall of long-time Egyptian President Hosni Mubarak, followed by the installation of a Muslim brotherhood President, Mohammed Morsi, and then his ouster in June 2013, turning leadership over to army chief Abdel Fatah el-Sisi. Later, in June 2014 after el-Sisi resigned from the military, he was elected virtually unopposed and presently serves as Egyptian president. Meanwhile, Morsi sits in prison, having been sentenced to death – probably unjustly – by an Egyptian court. Morsi's plight continues to ignite protests by Egyptian Muslims. Turkey's President Recep Tayyip Erdoğan has been outspoken about Morsi's fate, asserting that such a travesty of justice would never be tolerated in Western courts. While there is no love loss by this author in

**Mohammed Morsi,
Egypt's Former President in Prison**

respect to the Muslim Brotherhood, there remains a legitimate question about whether justice has been served and whether it is wise for the Egyptian regime to keep Morsi imprisoned and facing death.

Nine months after the sacrificial "first fire" of Ben Ali in Tunisia, Libyan President Muammar Gadhafi was assassinated trying to escape rebel forces outside Tripoli (20 October 2011). Rumors regarding his fate involve considerable intrigue. Some accounts allege that the coalition (France, England, and the United States) overthrew Gadhafi's government to confiscate Libya's gold. Additionally, it has been openly admitted by U.S. officials that the CIA was intricate to the planning of his overthrow ostensibly to enact justice for Gadhafi's criminal actions targeting the West, including planning and carrying out various bombings; most notably Pan Am Flight 103, which crashed in Lockerbie, Scotland (22 December, 1988) after a bomb planted by Libyan terrorists exploded in its cargo hold.

Post-Gadhafi, chaos reigns throughout Libya. Russian President Vladimir Putin points to Libya as what he contends is a classic example of CIA covert action and an expression of "standard" destructive American foreign policy in the Middle East. This accusation, unlike many others emanating from Russia, can no longer be so easily dismissed.

Today we find Syrian President Bashar al-Assad at the center of controversy for his government's murder of perhaps 250,000 Syrian civilians. But the U.S. joined the fight against Assad, i.e., the Syrian civil war, only in July 2014 after ISIS rebels beheaded American journalist James Foley (as recorded in an infamous and gruesome video). For two years before this event, despite recommendations from local American ambassadors, the U.S. remained reluctant to provide support to Syrian rebels. Afterwards, the current U.S. administration commenced bombing ISIS locations and began half-heartedly training moderate Syrian rebels (aka The Free Syrian Army - FSA) in Turkey and Jordan. Fearing that President Bashar would meet a similar fate to Gadhafi, Vladimir Putin intervened in the Syrian civil war to support Assad, justifying his actions as measures meant to "provide stabilization to the region." His claim was that American had brought chaos to the region; he would reinforce law and order.

Of course, it was the Syrian civil war, and ISIS attacks which were the fundamental crises spurring the massive migration of over one million refugees, flooding Europe during 2015. The repercussions of this unplanned immigration will have vast implications, reshaping European politics and culture for the remainder of this century. Meanwhile, despite ten thousand sorties completed by coalition and Russian forces, ISIS still advances its global terrorist threat. The recent San Bernardino murders of 14 U.S. citizens provide a grim reminder. As long as ISIS remains intact, it will inspire future acts of terror. As I complete this study, yet another series of terror attacks have been carried out in Brussels, Belgium. Just two weeks prior, attacks also occurred in Turkey.

Speaking of Turkey, it has been on the cusp of war with Russia after shooting down a Russian fighter on November 24, 2015, that Turkey claims was invading Turkish airspace. Never mind that Turkey was guilty of using the Syrian civil war as an excuse to continue its assault on Kurdish "rebels" – who had demonstrated their valuable ability to successfully engage and defeat ISIS. Under the disguise of attacking ISIS, Turkey repeatedly bombed Kurdish positions reducing the effectiveness of the overall coalition effort against jihadi extremists. It seems that teaming with Turkey is no walk in the park.

Russian officials have accused Turkey of covertly supporting ISIS, specifically alleging that Turkish President Erdoğan and his son are profiting from ISIS oil sales. Purportedly, Turkey allows the free flow of ISIS oil across its border and through its territory (oil is drawn from producing oil platforms in western Iraq and trucked through Turkey). Whether or not Turkey aids and abets ISIS, ISIS "gleans" over a *million dollars daily* in the sale of oil, self-financing its murderous activities. ISIS no longer needs (but nonetheless still receives) millions of dollars in donations from Sunni billionaires in Saudi Arabia and Qatar. The U.S. should be thinking, "With allies like these…"

## U.S. Abrogation of Responsibility for the Middle East

Initially President Obama characterized ISIS as Al-Qaeda's "JV" (Junior Varsity). However, like many other foreign policy assessments of this administration, ISIS has not gone quietly into that good night. As I noted in *The Next Great War in the Middle East,* the real battle in the Middle East goes far beyond rebel bands and terrorist organizations. It involves the three-century-old so-called "Great Game" between Russia and the West (first played by the British Empire and now, over the past 70 years, quarterbacked by the U.S.) However, the current administration has played the game with less enthusiasm over the past five years and the consequences are monumental.

Who will ultimately control the Middle East? The U.S. brags it stands as the "sole global superpower" inferring Russia is just a "regional power". The cold hard fact is that *Russian power only need be projected in the Middle East for Russia to dominate global politics.* Because of its vast reserves of fossil fuels, the "Levant" comprises the "choke point" for a majority of the world's energy needs and thus, *global* economics. Being the sole global superpower and possessing the capability to project power around the globe, really just means the U.S. is spread too thin to "go all in" against Russia in the Middle East. Having chosen to be a global policeman, the U.S. cannot be equally effective in every conflict. In the days of "sequestration", the price of maintaining peace is a budget breaker. The British learned this after World War I. The U.S. has yet to arrive at the same inevitable conclusion.

The recent release of the film *13 Hours* highlights the story of CIA contractors attempting to prevent the murder of American diplomat J. Christopher Stevens, killed in Benghazi, Libya, on September 12, 2012. The U.S. government may never acknowledge the truth behind the story, but it appears that the U.S. Executive Branch was moving guns from Libya (utilizing Gaddafi's enormous cache of weapons) through Turkey to rebels in Syria. Exactly which groups were the intended recipients became murky as time went own. Soon, however, the guns were finding their way into the hands of Jabhat al-Nusra, the Syrian affiliate of Al-Qaeda, America's former Public Enemy Number One. Less provable was that these weapons were winding up in the hands of ISIS with the knowledge of the CIA, the State Department, and the Pentagon.

What developed then, according to highly regarded (but sometimes controversial) reporter Seymour Hersh, in effect amounted to a quiet coups d'état within the United States. According to Hersh, The Pentagon grew increasingly distressed about White House plans to arm Syrian

**Seymour Hersh, Investigative Journalist**

rebels even through the evidence was that Al-Qaeda and ISIS were the real beneficiaries of the armaments originating in the U.S. and then later, from Gadhafi's cache of weapons in Libya.

Hersh tells us that The Joint Chiefs communicated "military to military" with their counterparts in Russia, Germany, and Israel to provide actionable intelligence useful to Assad in his war against Syrian rebel forces (those backed by the CIA and the White House). As a result it has become all too clear just how confused U.S. strategy in the Middle East is. It has gone so far off course as to pit the U.S. against itself – the Pentagon has been covertly fighting against the CIA and White House in the sands of Iraq and Syria. To assess the situation as a total unacceptable mess constitutes a colossal understatement. Hersh provides details in his January 7, 2016 *London Review of Books* article. Says Hersh:

> The military's resistance dates back to the summer of 2013, when a highly classified assessment, put together by the Defense Intelligence Agency (DIA) and the Joint Chiefs of Staff, then led by General Martin Dempsey, forecast that the fall of the Assad regime would lead to chaos and, potentially, to Syria's takeover by jihadi extremists, much as was then happening in Libya. A former senior adviser to the Joint Chiefs told me that the document was an 'all-source' appraisal, drawing on information from signals, satellite and human intelligence, and took a dim view of the Obama administration's insistence on continuing to finance and arm the so-called moderate rebel groups. By then, the CIA had been conspiring for more than a year with allies in the UK, Saudi Arabia and Qatar to ship guns and goods – to be used for the overthrow of Assad – from Libya, via Turkey, into Syria. The new intelligence estimate singled out Turkey as a major impediment to Obama's Syria policy. The document showed, the adviser said, 'that what was started as a covert US programme to arm and support the moderate rebels fighting Assad had been co-opted by Turkey, and had morphed into an across-the-board technical, arms and logistical programme for all of the opposition, including Jabhat al-Nusra and Islamic State. The so-called moderates had evaporated and the Free Syrian Army was a rump group stationed at an airbase in Turkey.' The assessment was bleak: there was no viable 'moderate' opposition to Assad, and the US was arming extremists.

For those who watch the geopolitical developments in the Middle East, and the prospects that Russia may be intensifying its presence there "for the long haul", the soundings today return with proof we are about to reach the destructive shores of what is known among Bible prophecy aficionados as the War of Gog and Magog (Ezekiel 38-39). In this War, Gog (who this author believes is Russia and not Turkey) will assemble a massive war effort against Israel, throwing the war into global conflict. As I argue in *"The Next Great War"* mentioned earlier, *the U.S., the U.K., and Saudi Arabia will all likely face attack;* potentially including nuclear missile assaults for U.S. citizens on its homeland.

So where are we today? The U.S. appears to have lost its grip in the region. The fact that the U.S. sided with Iran through the recent "treaty" (the so-called July 14, 2015 "nuclear deal"), and therefore threw in with the Shia against moderate Sunni regimes (like Jordan and long-time friends Egypt and Saudi Arabia), does not bode well for American influence in the region. Perhaps the current administration thought that picking "Persia" over Israel would win the U.S. points. In the end, the U.S. aided Russia's efforts to strengthen Iran and carry the day across the so-called "Fertile Crescent." Should this conclude with a betrayal of Israel (which now seems inevitable), I do not need to tell my readers that the U.S. will literally call down fire from heaven upon itself. The Daughter of Babylon will indeed become as Sodom and Gomorrah. *"And Babylon, the glory of kingdoms, the beauty of the Chaldees' excellency, shall be as when God overthrew Sodom and Gomorrah."* (Isaiah, 13:19, see also Jeremiah 49:18, 50:40)

## Conclusion: The Confrontation of the Century Lies Just Ahead

Exactly where this will lead seems clear enough to this author although for the time being the precise pathway remains imperceptible. In the months ahead and over the next year or two, expect Russia to gain increased domination of the region (mostly by proxy), controlling more and more of the Middle Eastern oilfields, eventually driving oil prices higher (despite the amazingly low prices today), as Putin inevitably runs a gambit to corner the market on petroleum and natural gas. His recent partial withdraw from Syria does not alter the equation.

We should also recognize that Ukraine, like the Middle East, is crucial to Russian interests since almost all pipelines transporting Russian oil and natural gas to Europe pass through this country which lies right in the middle between supplier and consumer (see map from the prior section). Make note it is not just the perennial Russian naval base in Crimea at Sevastopol that demands Moscow's attention; the network of pipelines crisscrossing the Ukraine is just as vital to Russia.

Over 40 years ago noted Bible prophecy scholar, the late John F. Walvoord wrote a prescient piece entitled, *Armageddon, Oil, and the Middle East Crisis* (1974). In his book he predicted oil would be the "hook in the jaws" for Gog (Russia) that would bring it into confrontation with Israel. Despite myriad obstacles and changes of direction since then, the destination Walvoord predicted for Russia hasn't changed one iota. As Grant Jeffrey phrased it, Russia will still keep its "appointment with destiny."

> *"So will I make my holy name known in the midst of my people Israel; and I will not let them pollute my holy name any more: and the heathen shall know that I am the LORD, the Holy One in Israel."* (Ezekiel 39:7)

Five years of Arab Spring have propelled us far down the path toward this prophetic fulfillment. The pace will only accelerate.

# Appendix II:
# Historical References to Gog and Magog

THE INFORMATION IS THIS APPENDIX was developed from the fine research presented by Tim Osterholm and made available without copyright at SoundChristian.com. My contribution is to organize and recap portions of his research in a tabular format with a focus on sources and the timing of their reference. It is ordered by the most ancient reference to most current.

| Date of Reference | What Person or Group Asserted | What was Stated and the Implications of the Information |
|---|---|---|
| From the 9th century BC | Assyrian inscriptions | Earliest record of Magog, "Mat Gugi" – "country of the Gugu." Magogians and Scythians became one people. |
| Beginning of 9th century BC | **Homer**, from the *Iliad* | *Hippo-Molgoi* (Greek for horse and *Molgoi* perhaps a transliteration of Magog). "Scythian drinkers of mare milk.' Domesticators of horses. |
| 9th century BC | According to Osterholm: | *Alans* and *Sarmatians* lived near the Caspian Sea, collectively called Scythians. |
| Beginning of 7th century BC | Assyrian records | Ashkenaz was recorded as *Ishkuzai*, a people "pouring in from the north" (of Assyria – north of Mesopotamia). |
| 7th century BC | **Hesiod**, father of Greek didactic poetry | Identified Magog with Scythians living in southern Russia. Likely derived his opinion from a Thracian tribe, the Colchians who described the region as "Gog-chasan" or "Gog-hasan" (Arabic "Gog-i-hisn") meaning "fortress of Gog". |
| 7th century BC - 5th century BC | "Scholars speculate" according to Osterholm | Gog-chasan, translated by Greeks as Gogasus or **Caucasus**, apparent origin of the name of this mountain range between the Black and Caspian Seas. |
| 6th century BC | Thousands of burials of Magogians / Scythians | Bodies found in *Chilikta Valley*, East Kazakhstan stretching all the way to Mongolia, dating to this period. |
| 6th century BC | **Ezekiel**, Hebrew prophet and priest | In the last days, Gog from the land of Magog will lead Meschech, Tubal, Gomer, Persia, and Beth-Togarmah against Israel. Whether 'Russia' is included is disputed. |
| 5th century BC | **Herodotus**, "the father of history" | Mentions the *Gargarians* living in the Caucasus, aka *Georgi* or *Gorgene*, from which the name *Georgia* probably originated. |
| 5th century BC – claiming 10th century BC data | **Herodotus** | Wrote of 3 tribes of *Scythians*, living in the territory north of the Black Sea – they terrorized the southern steppes of Russia *beginning in the 10th century BC*. |
| 5th century BC – claiming 10th century BC data | **Herodotus** | "Wandering Scythians once dwelt in Asia where that warred with the *Massagetae* (Magogites)" [already is Asia] and then left their homes, crossed the Caucasus, and displaced the *Gomerites* living in Anatolia (Turkey). [Note: They moved from east back to the west.] |
| 5th century BC | "Many scholars suggest" according to Osterholm: | **Great Wall of China** built to keep out the Magogians / Scythians. This indicates that Magogians were a force to deal with by the 5th century B.C. in *eastern* Asia. |

| 4th century BC | Chinese histories | *Tungu* tribes in the far west, were a bow-wielding, horse-archer civilization. They occupied northern Siberia. Huns saw them as a "filthy, unclean nomadic people". |
|---|---|---|
| 1st century BC | **Philo of Alexandria** Greek and Jewish philosopher | Identified Magog with southern Russia. |
| 1st century AD | **Strabo,** Greek historian | Makes mention of Homer's Hippo-Molgoi, likely reference to Magog and Scythians. |
| 1st century AD | **Strabo,** Greek historian, 17 vol. set, *Geographica*. *Ethnic origin, Georgian.* | Mentions *Gogarene* as a region in present-day Armenia and Georgia. Scholars say *Gogarene* "best preserved name of Magog" |
| 1st century AD | **Flavius Josephus** Jewish and Roman historian | *Magogites* (Magogians) were called "Scythians" by the Greeks. Togarmah was the father of the Phrygians |
| 2nd century AD | **Aelius Herodianus** - Greek / Roman scholar | Called the region *Gogarene* |
| 4th century AD | **Dionysius Periegetes,** a Greek geographer | Notes Huns (uni), *Caspii, Massagets, Sacii, Alani,* and *Scyths* lived in northern Europe. |
| Late 4th century AD | **Jerome** (translator of the Vulgate, Catholic Bible) | "The Jews of this age understood by Magog the vast and innumerable nations of Scythia, about Mount Caucasus, and the Palus Maeotis (Latin for Maeotis Sea), stretching along the Caspian Sea to India." Also, he saw Togarmah as father to the Phrygians. |
| 5th century AD | **Achoucha Gougarqtzi** – a viceroy in the region | Name he gave himself; translation would be "Arshusha of *Gogarene*) |
| 6th century AD | **Stephen of Byzantium**, a geographer | Called the region *Gogarene*. |
| Today | Common name used by modern-day Turks | Turks call Georgia "*Gurgistan*". |
| Today | **Tim Osterholm** | "The tribes of Magogians and Scythians would become many of the great confederations of steppe warriors… mingling with others not of the same race, developing ethnic [Eurasian mixtures]." |
| Today | Official Turkish history (acc. to Osterholm) | Hun Empire was the first Turkish state. "The Tungus, Ruruans, and Turks were known as a Siberian Hunnic people who spoke similar Altaic languages." |
| Today | Official Turkish history (acc. To Osterholm) | The 6th century Tartars eventually were subjugated by the *Khitans* (Kitans), then overthrown by the Uyghurs, then they by the *Kirghiz*. Late 10th century, there arose a large Turkish tribe, the *Kiniks*. The *Ghuzz* Turks would arise from the Kiniks. Ghuzz fathered *Seljuk* whose offspring, *Sultan Osman Ghazi (Osman I)* founded the Ottoman Empire in the 11th century. |

Osterholm provides this summation:

> There are many evidences that link Turks, Huns and Mongols from their earliest formations as tribes of Magogians and Scythians: (1) their Ural-Altaic languages; (2) their use of Runic inscriptions; (3) their coming from the north; and (4) their extensive use of horses and archery. Ezekiel describes them in similar terms: Ezekiel 38:4, "I will turn you around, put hooks in your jaws and bring you out with your whole army – *your horses, your horsemen fully armed, and a great horde with large and small shields, all of them brandishing their swords.*" Ezekiel 39:2-3, "I will turn you around and drag you along. I will bring you from the *far north* and send you against the mountains of Israel. Then I will *strike your bow* from your left hand and *make your arrows drop* from your right hand."
>
> Similarities remain in the languages of Mongolian, Tungusic and Turkic to this day, having many words in common. These Ural-Altaic languages have been historically considered "Scythian" or "Tatar" languages, which make up some 40 languages spoken by about 100 million people. Examples include Turkish, Kazakh, Kirghiz, Bashkir, Azerbaijani, Uzbek, Samoyed, Oirat, Kalmyk, and Mogol, plus similar languages spoken by peoples living between the Black and Caspian seas. Other language families, including Finno-Ugric (Finnish, Hungarian) and Balto-Slavic (Russian, Ukrainian, Czech) have affinities to the Ural-Altaic language family.
>
> We know the early Huns and Mongols were a nomadic Siberian horse-riding peoples who would eventually travel west to conquer, subsequently leaving Asian tribes to populate the region known today as Mongolia. We also know that the Huns became today's Turks (Turkic peoples), and the Scythians are today's Russians. As noted earlier, these people groups would eventually populate present-day Eurasia, including Russia, Siberia, the numerous republics north of Israel as precisely described in Ezekiel 38 and 39. Gog and Magog's descendants are today the peoples of those regions. Recent genetic research shows that many of the great confederations of early Asian steppe war tribes were not entirely of the same race, but rather tended to be ethnic mixtures of the Turkic, Tungus, Mongolian, and in many cases Scythian and Iranian (note that today more than 90% of these people groups are Muslim).

The evidence of scholarly research demonstrates that Magog was already widely dispersed throughout Asia at the time of Ezekiel. That Magog, Meshech and Tubal were connected with place names in Turkey is not surprising since all of humanity, after Noah's flood, originated in Turkey and Armenia. It was from there that they heeded the Lord's command to be "fruitful and multiply and replenish the earth".

As I presented in considerable detail in *The Next Great War in the Middle East*, chapter 9, "The Sons of Japheth", by Ezekiel's day humanity was nearing the end of its second millennium AFTER the flood (almost 2,000 years later). Ezekiel would likely have understood the tribal names he listed representing peoples living to the northeast, north, and northwest of Babylon and Persia. Whether he identified them solely as residents of Anatolia *only* is, in my opinion, highly unlikely. Magog, Meschech, Tubal, Gomer, Beth-Togarmah represented Gentiles living beyond the Caucasus. The sons of Japheth occupied all of Europe, most of Asia, and even much of the "New World" when Ezekiel penned his prophecies. No one can know with any certainty what Ezekiel understood at the time of his prophecy, nor can we say that what he knew was crucial to the prophecy he penned as the words were given him by the Spirit. But it is highly probable the educated in his day understood that the descendants of these tribes Ezekiel identified lived throughout Europe and Asia to the farthest seas to the east, west, and to the north!

**Tim Osterholm's references from soundchristian.com, "Gog and Magog."**

Osterholm notes the following are Google Downloadable Digitized Books:

*Colchians:* "The History of Herodotus: A New English Version," George Rawlinson, Henry Rawlinson, et al, published 1860

*Gog-hasan / Gogarene / Maiotis:* "The Millennium of the Apocalypse" George Bush, published 1842

*Scythians:* "The Geography of Herodotus, Developed, Explained and Illustrated from Modern Researches and Discoveries," published 1854

*Scythians:* "Larcher's Notes on Herodotus: Historical and Critical Comments on the History of Herodotus, with a Chronological Table, Volume II," published 1844

*Hiongnu / Huns:* "Universal History," Johann Mueller, published 1837

*Ta-Ta / Tartars:* "The Journey of William of Rubruck to the Eastern Parts of the World, 1253-55," published 1900

Other Books/Publications Utilized:

"Genghis Khan: His Life and Legacy," Paul Ratchnevsky, Thomas Nivison Haining, published 1991

"The Secret History of the Mongols: A Mongolian Epic Chronicle of the Thirteenth Century," translated by Igor De Rachewiltz, published 2006

"Who is Gog and Where is Magog?," Haskell Rycroft, published 2010

"The Magog Invasion," Chuck Missler, published 1996

"Foes from the Northern Frontier: Invading Hordes from the Russian Steppes," Edwin Yamaguchi, published 1982

"A General, Historical, and Topographical Description of Mount Caucasus, Volumes I & II," Jacob Reineggs, et al, translated & published 2001

Websites referenced by Osterholm:

http://www.republicanchina.org/Mongols.html

http://www.accd.edu/sac/history/keller/Mongols/empsub1.html

Recommended Maps by Osterholm:

http://www.worldhistorymaps.info/

About the author:

## S. DOUGLAS WOODWARD

is the author of twelve books and contributor to many others. He encourages his followers to communicate with him via his email account and can reached at *doug@faith-happens.com*. His web site is *www.faith-happens.com*. He blogs almost every day at facebook.com/s douglas woodward.

Doug appears frequently on television and radio programs and his interviews may be found on YouTube and Vimeo by searching for Doug Woodward. You will see Doug frequently hosting Prophecy in the News.

His books can be purchased at Amazon and are available in print and electronic formats such as Kindle, iBook, and Nook.

# ENDNOTES

[1] Futurism constitutes a popular belief among most evangelical Bible prophecy scholars and students. Futurism contends that almost half of the Bible's prophecies await future fulfillment. These "yet to be fulfilled" prophecies are almost entirely connected to the Second Advent of Christ aka the Apocalypse (and popularly known as "Armageddon").

[2] I presume this book published by WND Books is a reworked version of Joel's earlier 2006 book, *Antichrist: Islam's Awaited Messiah*.

[3] Shoebat denies that he has reduced the scope of end time's prophecy to a regional matter. I believe the particulars of his argument as well as the effective impact of his teaching, testifies otherwise.

[4] As I have explained in several of my books, beginning with my first book, Are We Living in the Last Days, saying the bible is literally true confuses the fact that the Bible uses metaphors, similes, hyperbole, personification, and virtually all poetic devices. There are many images and allegories. The issue is whether the prophet in question offered a prophecy and clearly indicated his prediction would come to pass as an historical event, in the future, in the realm in which we live which we describe today (post-Einstein) as "space-time".

[5] This makes me think of the lyrics of the song, "Why Can't We be Friends" by War. It is difficult to be friends when one of the two wants to assassinate the other. At best, it takes two willing people to be friends and two who are willing to act in good faith.

[6] See http://www.answering-islam.org/authors/thomas/moderate_islam.html for an article by Jacob Thomas:

On 22 January 2011, The Wall Street Journal published a review of two new books on **"the War on Terror."**[1] The reviewer, Michael B. Mukasey[2] entitled his review: **"America's Most Wanted: Two new books about the war on terror say that Osama bin Laden has achieved his goal — and we haven't."**

> Near the end of the review, Mr. Mukasey remarked: "Finally, consider Mr. Bergen's assertion that 'mainstream Islam' is rejecting al Qaeda and that the 9/11 attack was 'un-Islamic,' a judgment that fails twice over, including once on his own evidence. If by "mainstream Islam" Mr. Bergen means moderate Islam, there is no such thing. There are many moderate Muslims, but there is simply no body of doctrine within Islam that provides a principled basis for condemning the 9/11 attacks."

> I would like to add some further thoughts on his observation that "If by 'mainstream Islam' Mr. Bergen means moderate Islam, there is no such thing. There are many moderate Muslims, but there is simply no body of doctrine within Islam that provides a principled basis for condemning the 9/11 attacks."

> The term **"Moderate Muslim"** is a Western construct and has no equivalent phrase in contemporary Arabic. The use of it by Westerners reflects their assumption that there surely must exist Muslims who differ with their radical brothers in the faith who hanker after imposing Islam's legal system known as **Shariah.** I prefer to use the terminology that is current in the contemporary Arab-Muslim world describing non-Islamist or **salafist** [salafist equals *fundamentalist* Islam] thought such as **"reformist"," "secular"** or **"modernizing"**. For instance, Arabic-language websites such as **www.elaph.com** routinely post articles that boldly and critically interact with classical Islam. These thinkers and writers dream of a humane version of Islam that is compatible with the modern world would arise. However, the verdict of the last 1400 years does not substantiate that hope!

[7] "In biblical studies, pseudepigrapha refer particularly to works which purport to be written by noted authorities in either the Old and New Testaments or by persons involved in Jewish or Christian religious study or history. These works can also be written about biblical matters, often in such a way that they appear to be as authoritative as works which have been included in the many versions of the Judeo-Christian scriptures. Eusebius of Caesarea indicates this usage dates back at least to Serapion, bishop of Antioch whom Eusebius records as having said: "But those writings which are falsely inscribed with their name (pseudepigrapha), we as experienced persons reject...."

Many such works were also referred to as Apocrypha, which originally connoted "secret writings", those that were rejected for liturgical public reading. An example of a text that is both apocryphal and pseudepigraphical is the Odes of Solomon. It is considered pseudepigraphical because it was not actually written by Solomon but instead is a collection of early Christian (first to second century) hymns and poems, originally written not in Hebrew, and apocryphal because they were not accepted in either the Tanakh or the New Testament." See https://en.wikipedia.org/wiki/Pseudepigrapha.

[8] See White, Chris (2015-04-06). *The Islamic Antichrist Debunked: A Comprehensive Critique of the Muslim Antichrist Theory,* CWM Publishing. Kindle Edition.

[9] Wikipedia provides a nice article on the subject. Here is the summary citation: "Last Roman Emperor or Last World Emperor is a figure of medieval European legend, which developed as an aspect of eschatology in the Catholic Church. The legend predicts that in the end times, a last emperor would appear on earth to reestablish the Holy Roman Empire and assume his function as biblical **katechon** who stalls the coming of the Antichrist. [2 Thessalonians 2:2-4, "the restrainer"] The legend first appears in the 7th-century apocalyptic text known as the Apocalypse of Pseudo-Methodius, and developed over the centuries, becoming particularly prominent in the 15th century. The notion of Great Catholic Monarch is related to it, as is the notion of the Angelic Pope." See https://en.wikipedia.org/wiki/Last_Roman_Emperor.

[10] "Before his death the Prophet cautioned his followers unequivocally that they should not worship or make idols of him like the followers of other Prophets did. He tirelessly educated them of his mortality and his being a man, except that he is the Messenger of God. The Qur'an unequivocally states: 'Say [O Prophet]: "I am but a mortal man like all of you" '(18:110). The Qur'an repeats this point several times." See http://mercyprophet.org/mul/node/3317.

[11] Ancient Assyria (circa 800-620 B.C.) did include a large portion of the Anatolia Peninsula (today's Turkey) although its "home base" was in northern Iraq, modern day Mosul. Islam would capture Anatolia in the eleventh century (1,700 years after Assyria was at the peak of its power); however, notably Constantinople (today's Istanbul), the capital of the Byzantine (Christian) Empire, was not conquered until 1453 another 700 years later. *Assyrians* were a people long before most *Syrians* were Christian or Muslim. The modern ear mixes these distinct peoples together as if they were one and the same.

[12] "The **Aeneid** (/ɨˈniːɪd/; Latin: *Aenēis* [aeˈneːɪs]) is a Latin epic poem, written by Virgil between 29 and 19 BC, that tells the legendary story of Aeneas, a Trojan who travelled to Italy, where he became the ancestor of the Romans." (See https://en.wikipedia.org/wiki/Aeneid).

[13] In chapter 10 of *The Next Great War in the Middle East*, I list a long list of scholars of Bible prophecy that have written extensively on the War of Gog and Magog and take a stand on when it occurs. Those who agree with me that the Gog/Magog War transpires BEFORE the Tribulation and especially the Great Tribulation includes important figures like Tim LaHaye and the late Grant Jeffrey just to name two.

[14] The "Lindsey/Jeffrey scenario" had America giving way to Europe due to immorality in America, and a robust European economy, not due to mutual destruction of the U.S. and Russia.

[15] Richardson holds to two kings only in Daniel 11, with the Antichrist and Gog comprising the same personage and identified in this passage as the King of the North. Conventional eschatology generally sees *three* kings once the Antichrist is introduced in Daniel 11:40 and thereafter. Then the King of the

North is distinct from the Antichrist and the King of the South. Exactly who these other two kings are is a matter for debate even among those who argue 'three kings' (yet future) are being discussed in Daniel's prophecy. I take up the issue in the last segment of Part II.

[16] See https://bible.org/seriespage/15-nations-millennium-and-eternal-state.

[17] From their website (http://nineveh.com/whoarewe.htm):

> The Assyrians of today are the descendants of the ancient Assyrian people, one of the earliest civilizations emerging in the Middle East, and have a history spanning over 6760 years.
>
> Assyrians are not Arabian or Arabs, we are not Kurdish, our religion is not Islam. The Assyrians are Christian, with our own unique language, culture and heritage. Although the Assyrian empire ended in 612 B.C., history is replete with recorded details of the continuous presence of the Assyrian people till the present time.
>
> Assyria, the land of the indigenous Assyrians, was partitioned after World War I by the victorious Allies, and is currently under occupation by Kurds, Turks, Arabs and Persians [a region from Turkey to Iran].
>
> The Assyrians are a stateless people and continue to be religiously and ethnically persecuted in the Middle East due to Islamic fundamentalism, Arabization and Kurdification policies, leading to land expropriations and forced emigration to the West. [Emphasis added]

[18] White, Chris, op. cit., Kindle Locations 529-531.

[19] See the article, "Edom: The Great Prophecy" by Gary Stearman, *Prophecy in the News Magazine*, April 2013. Stearman stated, "To the Jewish mind, Rome, Edom and the state religion of Roman Christianity came to be viewed as the descendants of the idolatries that had begun centuries earlier in ancient Babylon." The prophets likely intended [the use of the names] the 'Assyrian' or Asshur in the same mode as 'Edom'; that is, symbolizing the future enemy of Israel but not meant to be taken literally."

[20] From *Tehillim*, Vol. 2, p. 1329, cited by Stearman in *Prophecy in the News Magazine*, April 2013, p. 8.

[21] See https://en.wikipedia.org/wiki/Mamertine_Prison. I originally heard of this tradition through a presentation made by Hal Lindsey, but I do not recall the place and date of his talk. Note that Paul was beheaded and Peter crucified, albeit his manner of crucifixion was upside down. Peter was not a citizen of Rome. The sign in the photograph relates the tradition that both Paul and Peter were imprisoned there.

[22] In a personal conversation, Richardson indicated that it is certainly one of the greatest mysteries of the Bible.

[23] Ibid., Kindle Locations 1084-1085.

[24] Ibid., Kindle Locations 1109-1116. Citation from Shoebat and Richardson, *God's War on Terror: Islam, Prophecy and the Bible* (p. 396). Top Executive Media, Kindle Edition.

[25] Ibid., Kindle Locations 1144-1150.

[26] "The dickens" is a polite euphemism for "the devil" or stronger vulgar language in case you didn't know.

[27] Jordan and Egypt are non-combatants in this gambit, although according to the nations teamed with Gog in Ezekiel 38, some participants from Libya, Sudan, and Ethiopia sympathetic to the Shia cause must be involved to fulfill the prophecy to the letter. This would be an alternate explanation why the nations immediately surrounding Israel are not named in the War of Gog and Magog. If Daniel 11 (at least in part) provides prophecies yet to be fulfilled (and I am not certain that it does as I will explain later in the main text), Egypt appears in the Antichrist's war during the Tribulation period against the "king of the south". In any event, Egypt and Assyria (which consists in part of Syria and also other sections of the Middle East) are given places of honor in the Millennial Kingdom, which would also partially explain this configuration of alliances. John F. Walvoord makes this observation:

> A... prophecy is found in Isaiah 19:23-25 in reference to the future millennial kingdom: *"In that day shall there be a highway out of Egypt to Assyria, and the Assyrian shall come into Egypt,*

*and the Egyptian into Assyria, and the Egyptians shall serve with the Assyrians. In that day shall Israel be the third with Egypt and with Assyria, even a blessing in the midst of the land: Whom the Lord of hosts shall bless, saying, Blessed be Egypt my people, and Assyria the work of my hands, and Israel mine inheritance."*

It is evident from this passage that Israel's two most important neighbors in the millennial kingdom will be the peoples who inhabit the area of ancient Assyria to the northeast and Egypt to the southwest. In that day both Assyria and Egypt will be blessed along with Israel.

Keep in mind that while Syria is included in the lands of ancient Assyria, the two are not to be identified with one another. Assyria includes Syria, Iraq, and portions of Turkey and Iran.

[28] See http://www.prophezine.com/index.php?option=com_content&id=517%3Awhere-is-magog-meshech-and-tubal.

[29] White, Chris, op. cit., Kindle Locations 3646-3650.

[30] Ibid., Kindle Locations 3360-3366. Citation from Richardson: Richardson, Joel, *The Islamic Antichrist: The Shocking Truth about the Real Nature of the Beast* (p. 50), Midpoint Trade Books. Kindle Edition. Citation from Arif, Muhammad and Ibn Izzat Muhammad (2012-08-07). *Al Mahdi* (Kindle Locations 166-171). Dar Al Taqwa. Kindle Edition.

[31] Ibid.

[32] History suggests that Yose ben Halafta (d. 160 A.D.) a disciple of the famous Rabbi Akiva altered the Jewish calendar attempting to prove that Simon bar Kokhba, leader of the "second revolt" against Rome, was the Messiah (not Jesus of Nazareth). Simon was executed in 135 A.D. after setting up an independent Jewish state for two and one-half years. Akiva had blessed Simon declaring him to be the "star of the Scepter" or promised Messiah (from Numbers 24:17) The *Seder Olam Rabbah* (*The Book of the Order of the World*) compiled in the second century A.D. provides the calendric information mentioned here.

[33] From Obama's Jerusalem March 23, 2013 visit to Rosh Hashanah October 3, 2016, would be exactly, 1290 days, an interesting interval, but 1,260 would be much more interesting.

[34] See http://www.raptureforums.com/FeaturedCommentary/thethreekingsofdaniel11.cfm#.VvLrRnKT9V8.mailto

[35] It is interesting that this debate goes back all the way to Jerome and Porphyry in the fourth century. (Porphyry meant "clad in purple, a reference to his being from Tyre, i.e., Phoenicia).

[36] See http://www.herealittletherealittle.net/index.cfm?page_name=Daniel11. Updated January 2012.

[37] King Herod not only killed hundreds of babies in Judea, but had several of his own sons killed in his later years as well to protect his throne. Herod was never seriously considered for "Father of the Year".

[38] It is conceivable that Jesus and his earthly father Joseph worked on later building projects in Caesarea, as it was not far (about 30 miles) from Nazareth (this Herod died while Jesus was a child in Egypt). It was a major city for the time.

[39] In studying Daniel 11, it was noteworthy that Robert D. Culver and John F. Walvoord, two stalwart Futurists, mentioned Mauro's analysis but ignored entirely his analysis on King Herod in Daniel 11:36-45, both stating that no plausible theory for a historical "king" exists! I disagree. While I am an avowed futurist, the Preterist position on Daniel 11 is compelling and does not compromise seeing Daniel 12 fully in the future. It is at this point that Mauro's Preterist analysis goes awry and becomes incredulous; including a denial the bodily resurrection is prophesied in Daniel 12.

[40] Ari Yashar, "Putin withdrawing from Syria? Au contraire", *Arutz Sheva*, March 30, 2016, http://www.israelnationalnews.com/News/News.aspx/210096#.VwE2CMc4IoZ.